WORLD BANK TECHNICAL PAPER NUMBER 71

Reservoir Sedimentation

Impact, Extent, and Mitigation

K. Mahmood

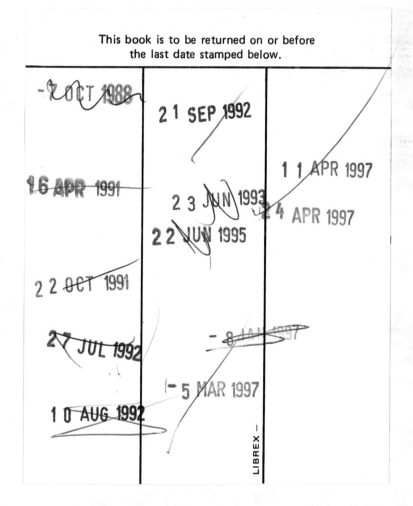
The World Bank
Washington, D.C.

The International Bank for Reconstruction
and Development THE WORLD BANK
1818 H Street, N.W.
Washington, D.C. 20433, U.S.A.

Technical Papers are not formal publications of the World Bank, and are circulated to encourage discussion and comment and to communicate the results of the Bank's work quickly to the development community; citation and the use of these papers should take account of their provisional character. The findings, interpretations, and conclusions expressed in this paper are entirely those of the author(s) and should not be attributed in any manner to the World Bank, to its affiliated organizations, or to members of its Board of Executive Directors or the countries they represent. Any maps that accompany the text have been prepared solely for the convenience of readers; the designations and presentation of material in them do not imply the expression of any opinion whatsoever on the part of the World Bank, its affiliates, or its Board or member countries concerning the legal status of any country, territory, city, or area or of the authorities thereof or concerning the delimitation of its boundaries or its national affiliation.

Because of the informality and to present the results of research with the least possible delay, the typescript has not been prepared in accordance with the procedures appropriate to formal printed texts, and the World Bank accepts no responsibility for errors. The publication is supplied at a token charge to defray part of the cost of manufacture and distribution.

The most recent World Bank publications are described in the catalog *New Publications*, a new edition of which is issued in the spring and fall of each year. The complete backlist of publications is shown in the annual *Index of Publications*, which contains an alphabetical title list and indexes of subjects, authors, and countries and regions; it is of value principally to libraries and institutional purchasers. The latest edition of each of these is available free of charge from the Publications Sales Unit, Department F, The World Bank, 1818 H Street, N.W., Washington, D.C. 20433, U.S.A., or from Publications, The World Bank, 66, avenue d'Iéna, 75116 Paris, France.

K. Mahmood is Professor of Engineering at The George Washington University, Washington, D.C., and a consultant to the World Bank.

Library of Congress Cataloging-in-Publication Data

```
Mahmood, H.
    Reservoir sedimentation.

    (World Bank technical paper, ISSN 0253-7494 ;
no. 71)
    Bibliography: p.
    1. Reservoir sedimentation.  2. Water resources
development.  I. Title.  II. Series.
TD396.M37  1987        628.1'32         87-23003
ISBN 0-8213-0952-8
```

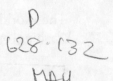

TABLE OF CONTENTS

List of Figures

List of Tables

PREFACE

This monograph deals with reservoir sedimentation--a subject of considerable import to the development of water resources in the world. Storage reservoirs are the primary line of defense against the vagaries of hydrological cycle. They protect against floods, as well as droughts. Add to this, the hydro-power, recreation, and navigation benefits of dams, and they emerge as the single most important structural factor in the world development. The present worth of all the dams in the world may well approach $600 billion. It is only prudent to evaluate their life against the insidious encroachment by sediment.

The average age of man made storage reservoirs in the world is estimated to be around 22 years. The loss of capacity due to siltation is already being felt at a number of structures. It is entirely possible that, unless ingenious solutions are developed, we will lose the struggle to enhance the available water resources.

Professor Mahmood has used his considerable experience in water resource and sedimentation engineering to develop a comprehensive and readable expose that can be easily followed by an interested and well informed non-specialist. His report should also help clear some of the commonly held misconceptions about reservoir sedimentation problems.

It is evident that the problem of reservoir sedimentation can be solved, at least to an extent, and that it will require greater consideration in the existing and future projects. With the $6 billion estimated annual loss there is sufficient incentive to start a concerted research and development effort in this field.

I wish to join the author in expressing our gratitude to many colleagues in the Bank who generously gave their time and wisdom to critically review the initial draft and made many valuable suggestions. I believe this monograph will be useful to development professionals around the world.

G. Edward Schuh
Director, Agriculture and
Rural Development Department

CHAPTER I

INTRODUCTION

Geological erosion is a part of drainage process. Erosion starts with the weathering of parent rock and ends with the deposit of eroded material in the delta. Sediment load, the clastic particles transported by streams is a concomitant part of surface water resources. It can be both an asset and a liability. In the context of storage reservoirs, it is a multifaceted liability.

Dams have been built for at least 5,000 years (Jansen, 1980) and, their functions have evolved with the developing needs of society. Most likely, the earliest dams were built to store water for domestic and agricultural water supply. With the onset of industrial era, hydro-power became a major reason for building dams. Presently, dams are built to serve many other functions, such as, flood control, navigation and recreation.

In all reservoirs created by dams, the volume of storage is a critical determinant of their efficacy. Excepting the low head irrigation dams--more appropriately called barrages, the utility of a reservoir diminishes as its storage capacity is reduced.

The downstream movement of a stream's sediment load is interrupted by reservoirs. Dams create potential energy by locally reducing the energy consumption of a stream flow. Smaller velocities upstream result in saving frictional head loss which is then concentrated as potential energy at the dam. The smaller velocities also mean that the sediment transport capacity within the reservoir is substantially reduced, if not altogether lost. The incoming sediment load starts depositing as soon as the stream enters the reservoir. From that point, the deposit extends both

1

upstream and downstream.

The upstream deposits are called "backwater deposits" in reference to the causative hydraulic phenomenon. The deposits within the reservoir are called "delta", "overbank" and "bottom-set beds" in accordance with their shape and location. The delta constitutes deposit of coarse material that is the first to drop out and bottom-set beds are fine sediments that may be transported farther downstream by density currents or otherwise. Overbank deposits comprise sediment that has settled over the former high bank or valley slopes. Engineering consequences of backwater and reservoir deposits are somewhat different. By raising the bed level of channel upstream of reservoir limit, backwater deposits create problems of flooding, waterlogging and non-beneficial use of water by phreatophytes. The physical impact of in-reservoir deposits is to reduce the volume of storage available for water.

As the sediment deposits approach the dam, they are released, to an extent, with the flow passing through outlet works and power turbines. Here, the sediment has another harmful effect. It abrades the structures it passes through.

There are other impacts related to dams. On the upstream side, the thermal regime of flow is changed so that the impounded water may become anaerobic or it may become hostile to the wildlife previously supported by the river. On the downstream side, the flow tends to pick up the sediment load from the stream bed leading to retrogression of channel bed and water level, erosion of banks, elimination of nutrients carried by the fine sediments, deterioration of channel morphology, increase in the hydraulic resistance of flow, elimination of oxbow lakes and reduction of wildlife food supply.

This monograph is concerned with the depletion of reservoir storage by sediment deposits. Its purpose is to provide a comprehensive review of the reservoir sedimentation problem; its associated processes, and the methods available to predict and control the loss of storage. It is addressed to engineers and planners involved in the planning, design and operation of storage reservoirs. Environmental impacts of storage reservoirs, other than those presented herein, are discussed in Goodland (1985). Physical impacts of dams on the downstream river channel are covered in Williams and Wolman (1984) and Harrison and Mellema (1982).

Chapter II starts with an assessment of the problem and its economic implications. Physical concepts of erosion and sedimentation related to drainage basins are introduced in Chapter III. This chapter contains considerable discussion of sediment production and transport out of drainage basins. Current estimates of sediment load in some 62 basins from around the world are presented, more to indicate geographic distribution of problem and to define range of sediment loads that may be expected. Man's impact on sediment load in rivers and the role played by infrequent natural events like floods, hurricanes and earthquakes are also described. Finally, some special conditions relating to the measurement of sediment load in rivers, that must be carried out to provide design information, are briefly discussed. Chapter IV deals with important properties of sediment particles and sedimentation processes within the reservoirs. These are: particle size, critical conditions of entrainment, delta formation, bottom-set deposits and density currents. State-of-the-art methods for predicting the sedimentation aspects of design are presented in Chapter V. Chapter VI deals with the ultimate question of what can be done to mitigate the impact of sedimentation on reservoir life. Three categories of methods which are available to combat reservoir sedimentation—from watershed management to dredging, are discussed in regard to their scope and limitations. Case histories are used in support of their evaluation.

Chapter VII summarizes the main conclusions and makes recommendations for future research and development studies which are needed. It is emphasized that the economic cost of reservoir sedimentation in the world is large and that it will worsen in the future, so that vigorous research on this problem is urgently needed.

CHAPTER II

MAGNITUDE OF THE PROBLEM

In regard to their temporal distribution, surface water resources can be divided into two classes: base flow and direct runoff. Base flow is the minimum available over a yearly cycle and the direct runoff is the fluctuating component which is only available during a part of the year. The base flow comes from the groundwater and due to its assuredness is the most valuable component. One of the principal aims of water resource development is to augment the base flow at a site. This can be economically and reliably achieved by temporarily storing the direct runoff in man-made reservoirs.

In its natural state, the base flow constitutes about 36 percent of the world-wide surface runoff and dams have been historically built by man to regulate direct runoff into base flow. There are, of course, other benefits associated with flow regulation. For example, the magnitude of flood peak is reduced and the potential energy created by water impoundment can be used to generate power.

According to a 1974 world estimate (UNESCO, 1978 - Table 8), the volume of all storage reservoirs with gross capacities of 5 km^3 and above, amounts to 4,050 km^3. This includes the projects then under construction, which are assumed to be complete at this time(1986). Another 20 percent storage is estimated to lie in smaller reservoirs so that the gross volume of storage in the world is around 4,900 km^3 which is roughly 13 percent of total annual runoff. In the present context, gross capacity of a storage reservoir can be broadly divided into the usable and non-usable components. The latter is not available for base flow augmentation due to physical or regulatory constraints or due to its prior allocation to other uses such as flood control. Usable storage is the storage volume used to retain direct runoff for later release. The ratio of usable to gross capacity of reservoirs varies in different geographical regions between 38 to 59 percent with a storage weighted world average of around 50 percent. The usable capacity is nearly used once every year. Using a conservative estimate of base runoff augmentation equal to 40 percent of gross capacity, the net augmentation of world's base flow by storage reservoirs is estimated to be about 16 percent. See Table 2-1.

Beginning with the 1950's, construction of large reservoirs has experienced a major growth in the world. In fact, all of the reservoirs with a capacity over 50 km^3 were constructed after 1950. During the two decades of 50's and 60's, the gross storage capacity in the world increased by 25 time (UNESCO, 1978). In the two-year period, 1966-68 alone, about 375 km^3 of storage were added to the world total (Mermal, 1970). Accelerated construction of reservoirs around the world is continuing and it is likely to do so in the future. Most scenarios of future developments in water resources agree that ultimately, say, by the mid-twenty-first century, all of the direct surface runoff must be stored by reservoirs or other methods. L'vovich (1979) estimates that by the turn of this century the usable storage will have to increase about 2.5-fold.

All reservoirs trap a part of sediment load transported by incoming flows and, therefore, experience a continual reduction of storage volume. The time rate of siltation in a reservoir varies with its design and the magnitude of sediment load. Hoover Dam, since its closure in 1935, has been losing gross capacity at an average rate of 0.3 percent per year. On the other hand, in Tarbela Dam, the average siltation rate is 1.5 percent per year, and that in Sanmexia Reservoir (China) is about 1.7 percent per year. There have been some notably high rates of siltation at other sites. The 76 m high Warsak Dam on Kabul River (Pakistan) lost 18 percent of

6

Table 2-1

ESTIMATED AUGMENTATION OF BASE FLOW BY STORAGE RESERVOIRS

Geographic Area	Annual Runoff Volume		Gross Reservoir Capacity			Augmentation of Base Flow	
	Total	Natural Base Flow	Volume	% of World	% of total Runoff	Volume	% of Natural Base Flow
	(km³)	(km³)	(km³)			(km³)	
North America	5,950	1,900	975	20.0	16.4	390	23.1
Asia	13,190	3,440	1,770	36.3	13.4	710	23.2
Africa	4,225	1,500	1,280	26.2	30.3	510	38.7
So. America	10,380	3,740	340	7.0	3.3	140	4.0
Europe	3,100	1,125	450	9.2	14.5	180	17.8
Australia	1,965	465	65	1.3	3.3	30	6.5
World	38,810	12,170	4,880	100.0	12.6	1,960	16.1

Notes:
1. Annual runoff and base flow volumes after L'vovich (1979)

2. Gross capacity of all reservoirs in a region is estimated as 1.20 times capacity of reservoirs above 5 km³

3. Base flow augmentation based on 40 percent of gross capacity

4. Australia includes Tasmania, New Guinea and New Zealand

5. All figures rounded off and approximate

its storage volume in the very first year's operation.

World-wide data on the siltation of reservoirs is not available. It can be roughly estimated to be around 1 percent of the gross capacity per year. That is, on the global scale about 50 km^3 of capacity is being lost to sediment every year. The immediate implication of this loss is that the world capacity to augment base flow is being continuously eroded and that it must be replaced before any improvement can be made in the available water resources.

A part of the non-usable storage in reservoirs is specifically allocated to sediment storage. Generally, it lies below the elevation to which water can be drawn by gravity and it is then called the dead storage. The life of a storage is commonly, but erroneously, estimated as the volume of dead storage divided by the expected mean annual volume of sediment deposits. As explained in Chapter IV, such extrapolations are not valid. Reservoir sedimentation patterns are such that the usable capacity starts diminishing before all of the non-usable component is filled up with sediment.

On the basis of 1974 data on major world dams (capacity above 5 km^3, UNESCO, 1978) used with some extrapolations, the capacity weighted average age of world storages is presently (1986) estimated to be about 22 years. Total loss of usable capacity of world reservoirs to date is, thus, estimated to be around 540 km^3 with a resulting loss of base flow augmentation of around 220 km^3. This means that, around 1,100 km^3 of gross capacity have to be added at the present time to replace what has been lost so far. The cost of this replacement, at a modest rate of about $120 million per km^3, is $130 billion. This is equivalent to an annual loss of $6 billion in replacement costs alone. In many basins, additional sites are hard to find, and in general, remaining sites for storage reservoirs are more difficult and, hence, more expensive to develop. This is the magnitude of reservoir sedimentation problem in the world.

CHAPTER III

EROSION AND SEDIMENTATION IN DRAINAGE BASINS

Genesis of solid load in rivers lies in weathering of parent rock by chemical, mechanical and chemico-biological processes. Two different types of material result from weathering - the solution of mineral components and a crust of weathering. The former, appears as the dissolved solid content of river flow; is flushed almost continuously through the system and is largely irrelevant to the present context. Clastic sediment - our main concern in storage reservoirs, undergoes a series of mechanical processes like erosion, entrainment, transportation and deposition in its journey from the crust to the continental shelf and beyond. These processes are discontinuous and a sediment particle takes a series of transport and deposit steps. The latter sometimes being of the order of centuries.

Variables operative in weathering processes and those in subsequent mobilization by a transport agent - chiefly water, are theoretically independent, so that, sediment load at any location in a drainage basin may be limited by one set of processes or the other. Certain correlations, however, exist within the climatic variables and, they create a zonal pattern of sediment load in the world rivers. These processes and zonal estimates are the subject of this chapter. The purpose is to present a global picture of sediment load distribution in rivers including a discussion of man-made and natural factors, that may result in major deviations from otherwise well established patterns.

Weathering Processes

Weathering processes are classified as mechanical or chemical, depending on the dominance of forces that break up the parent rock. Mechanical processes imply disintegration by forces which overcome internal strength of rock such as in its shearing by glacier movement or the break up by freezing of water in the pores. The chemical processes are more complex. They start with the solution of easily dissolved salts under an alkaline environment followed by an acidic phase when the poorly soluble compounds also begin to migrate. Both processes are strongly dependent on climatic factors - availability of water, its phase and atmospheric temperature. When water is available in liquid phase and average annual temperatures are above 10° C, the chemical processes are dominant. When water is absent in liquid phase, as in arid to semi-arid, or glacial zones, the mechanical processes govern.

Strakhov (1967), has used the above line of reasoning to classify weathering into Humid, Arid and Glacial types. He estimates that the chemical weathering is most active in the Tropics - average annual temperatures of 24-26 degrees Centigrade and 1,200-3,000 mm rainfall, whereas, its rate in the temperate zones is only 2-5 percent of that in the Tropics. In arid zones, the temperature regime is favorable, but, water is scarce and organic matter is sparse so that chemical weathering becomes insignificant. Within each zone of weathering, other climatic and geologic factors, also, have important influences. For example, precipitation occurring only as episodic thunderstorms means that vegetal cover in the basin will be sparse and, hence, there will be a diminution of organic matter and chemical weathering. Among the geologic factors, tectonics is most important: with tectonic movements, mechanical weathering will be enhanced. With rapid movements, however, weathering crust does not develop.

Erosion

Erosion is defined as the detachment and removal of rock particles by water or by wind. The former is by far the most important agent. Weathering prepares the parent rock for erosion and rainfall acts as the chief agent for erosion. The combined effect of weathering and erosion is called mechanical denudation. The rate of mechanical denudation is measured in terms of the weight of clastic material removed per unit area and time, e.g., tons/km^2/yr or as the average thickness of crust layer removed over a unit time, e.g., meters/1,000 yr. When spatially applied over drainage basins, mechanical denudation is also measured by sediment yield which is defined as the mass rate of sediment outflow at a cross section of reference (e.g., as tons/km^2/yr).

Rate of mechanical denudation increases with all of the factors that add to the erosive power of rainfall such as higher relief, more intense rainfall and sparseness of vegetal cover. For this reason, within a homogeneous zone of weathering and relief, it has been possible to express sediment yield as the sole function of mean annual rainfall and temperature (Schumm, 1977). At low values of rainfall, the surface runoff is not enough to carry away the available material and beyond an optimal amount of rainfall, vegetal cover is well established to reduce the rate of erosion. Higher annual temperatures result in larger evapotranspiration losses so that a comparatively larger amount of rain is needed to produce the same density of vegetation and protection against erosion. Thus, in homogeneous zones of weathering, a maxima of sediment yield occurs at an intermediate amount of annual rain which is an increasing function of temperature.

Sediment Delivery Ratio

Removal of a detached sediment particle from its location occurs by its entrainment and transport by water. Not all of the detached particles are transported out of a basin. A majority is deposited on the slopes, bottom of slopes, in the channels and on the flood plains. The percentage of on-site eroded sediment per unit of basin area that is transported to a given downstream location is called: Sediment Delivery Ratio, D. It depends on the size and texture of eroded particles, relief and more importantly, on the areas of sediment storage available within the basin. For small basins, say of 0.002 km^2 area, the delivery ratio is generally assumed to be 100 percent. For larger basins, it is assumed to vary as

$$D = a / A^b \tag{3.1}$$

where a = constant, A = basin area and, b varies from 1/4 to 1/8. Values of D have been investigated up to basin areas of around 1,000 km^2.

Various attempts have been made in the past to express D as a power function of basin area and its morphometric parameters (e.g., Roehl, 1962). In view of the current knowledge on sediment storage within a drainage basin, these empirical relations must be considered site-specific, approximate and trend-indicative only. Also, there is evidence that the exponent b in Eq. (3.1) may, indeed, be an increasing function of A itself, so that, for basins of 10,000 km^2 and larger, the overall value of D may be much smaller than that indicated above. At the present state-of-the-art, it is not possible to predict values of D for large basins. These values, the details of sediment storage in a basin and its subsequent movement can only come through a long and difficult set of sedimentation measurements.

12

A number of studies have been made to measure short and long-term storage of sediment in river channels [e.g., Emmett and Leopold (1963), Foley and Sharp (1976), Emmett, et al (1980) and Meade, et al (1985)]. Similar studies at the level of drainage basins are, however, rare. A river channel has a largely confined domain. The drainage basin, on the other hand, presents a diffused sedimentation environment and is orders of magnitude more difficult to study.

Trimble (1983) has analyzed sediment balance data over 120 years period on 360 km^2 Coon Creek basin in Wisconsin. Over the first 85 years of the study period, accelerated erosion caused by forest clearing and agriculture, contributed about 2,080 t/km^2/yr of which 36% were retained on the hill slope, about 59% were stored in the valley and only about 5% (116t/km^2/yr) appeared at the mouth. During the next 37 years: the rate of erosion declined to 1,640t/km^2/yr due to improved land management practice; the rate of hill slope storage increased to account for 56 percent of supply; that in the valley storage declined to 38 percent and the outflow increased to 7 percent (110t/km^2/yr). Sediment delivery ratio in these data corresponds to an index of around 1/4 in Eq. (3.1), which is somewhat on the higher side and is probably caused by the ongoing saturation of sediment sinks within the basin. Hillslope and valley storage processes are dominant in these data. Even in this relatively small basin, the sediment yield at the mouth remains unaltered (in absolute terms) after 37 years of erosion control that reduced the rate of on-site erosion by more than 20 percent. In larger basin, the role of valley storage is expected to be larger.

Space and time variations of on-site erosion are largely dampened by storage within the basin which occurs wherever the transport capacity of flow declines. A drainage basin acts as a low pass filter between the on-site erosion and sediment yield. The strength of filter is related to factors that effect hydraulics of flow and sediment transport capacity such as, morphometry of the basin, topology of the drainage network, morphology of the channels, and behavioral size of particles constituting the sediment load. Drainage basins also exert a strong sorting of the particle size of sediment load. The average size of sediment particles at the mouth of a basin will be smaller than that of the eroded material. As shown by Rana, et al. (1973), sediment sorting occurs even in confined channel flows.

Coon Creek data also show that sediment sinks within a basin are more effective when the basin is first disturbed. The sinks, ultimately, tend to become sources as they are saturated, although most of the sediment trapped within a basin may never reappear at its mouth. Stream channels play a dual role in sediment delivery. Streambank erosion constitutes a significant source of sediment supply, [e.g., Missouri-Mississippi System, (Robbins, 1976) and Sacramento River, (Sing, 1986)] and to a large extent, the sediment delivery from a basin is controlled by the transport capacity of the channels. In the case of large storage reservoirs that trap nearly all of the incoming sediment load, stream channel erosion is the only source, other than the tributary inflows, for the sediment load that appears in the downstream flow.

In general, as the flow progresses along a drainage basin, it increases in volumetric rate, but declines in its sediment concentration and sediment particle size at a rate which is proportional to a small power of the drainage area. Some notable exceptions to this general pattern exist. The sediment load in Yellow River dramatically increases from a small fraction to about 1.5 billion tons/year as the river passes through the loess region some 350 km from its source, (Milliman and Meade, 1983). The mechanics of sediment storage and pick up within the drainage basin are well understood, but the results have not been adequately quantified.

World Wide Rates of Erosion and Delivery

Two different perspectives have been conventionally used in estimating world wide rates of erosion and sediment loads. One, dealing with on-site rates, is concerned with the sources of sediment generation and environmental consequences of erosion and the other, dealing with sediment delivery to the oceans (more correctly, near the mouths of basins discharging into oceans) for various geomorphic considerations. The difference between the two perspectives is sediment delivery ratio of the basins. As a rough estimate, only about one-tenth of the on-site erosion appears at the mouth of large basins.

Three recent estimates of world-wide suspended sediment delivery to oceans have been provided by: Strakhov (1967) - 12.7 billion tons; Holeman (1968) - 18.3 billion tons and Milliman and Meade (1983) - 13.5 billion tons per year. No comparable estimates exists for on-site erosion exist. But, one may assume that D is around 10 percent. In view of the variability of sampling techniques used in various countries and inadequacies of records such as errors and incompleteness, the above estimates are remarkably consistent.

Drainage basin data for 62 of the basins used by Milliman and Meade (1983) are summarized in Table 3-1. Besides their name, geographic location and size, three other parameters are listed for each basin: unit runoff, cm; sediment yield, t/km^2 and sediment concentration, ppm. The unit runoff measures the magnitude of surface runoff per unit area and is an indicator of water availability as a resource as well as an erosion/transport agent. Sediment yield, taken with an appropriate value of D, is an indicator of average on-site erosion rate in the basin and, sediment concentration is a measure of muddiness of water. These two parameters, in conjunction with reservoir design parameters, also determine the amount of sedimentation that will take place in a storage reservoir.

Table 3-1

ANNUAL WATER AND SEDIMENT YIELD OF WORLD'S RIVERS
AT OCEAN LEVEL

No	Continent	Country/ Economy	River	D. Area (mill km^2)	Runoff (cm)	Sediment (t/km^2)	Yield (ppm)
1	N. America	Canada	St. Lawrence	1.030	43	4	9
2	N. America	USA	Hudson	.020	60	50	83
3	N. America	USA	Mississippi	3.270	18	107	602
4	N. America	USA	Brazos	.110	6	145	2,286
5	N. America	Mexico	Colorado	.640	3	211	6,750
6	N. America	USA	Eel	.008	79	1,750	2,222
7	N. America	USA	Columbia	.670	37	12	32
8	N. America	Canada	Fraser	.220	51	91	179
9	N. America	USA	Yukon	.840	23	71	308
10	N. America	USA	Copper	.060	65	1,167	1,795
11	N. America	USA	Susitna	.050	80	500	625
12	N. America	Canada	Mackenzie	1.810	17	55	327
13	S. America	Peru	Chira	.020	25	2,000	8,000
14	S. America	Colombia	Magdelena	.240	99	917	928
15	S. America	Venezuela	Orinoco	.990	111	212	191
16	S. America	Brazil	Amazon	6.150	102	146	143
17	S. America	Brazil	Sao Francisco	.640	15	9	62
18	S. America	Argentina	La Plata	2.830	17	33	196
19	S. America	Argentina	Negro	.100	30	130	433
20	Europe	France	Rhone	.090	54	111	204

Table 3-1

ANNUAL WATER AND SEDIMENT YIELD OF WORLD'S RIVERS
AT OCEAN LEVEL - cont'd...

No	Continent	Country/ Economy	River	D. Area (mill km^2)	Runoff (cm)	Sediment (t/km^2)	Yield (ppm)
21	Europe	Italy	Po	.070	66	214	326
22	Europe	Romania	Danube	.810	25	83	325
23	Eu. Arctic	USSR	Yana	.220	13	14	103
24	Eu. Arctic	USSR	Ob	2.500	15	6	42
25	Eu. Arctic	USSR	Yenisei	2.580	22	5	23
26	Eu. Arctic	USSR	Sev. Dvina	.350	30	13	42
27	Eu. Arctic	USSR	Lena	2.500	21	5	23
28	Eu. Arctic	USSR	Kolyma	.640	11	9	85
29	Eu. Arctic	USSR	Indigirka	.360	15	39	255
30	Asia	USSR	Amur	1.850	18	28	160
31	Asia	China	Liaohe	.170	4	241	6,833
32	Asia	China	Daling	.020	5	1,800	36,000
33	Asia	China	Haiho	.050	4	1,620	40,500
34	Asia	China	Yellow	.770	6	1,403	22,041
35	Asia	China	Yangtze	1.940	46	246	531
36	Asia	China	Pearl	.440	69	157	228
37	Asia	Viet Nam	Hungho	.120	103	1,083	1,057
38	Asia	Viet Nam	Mekong	.790	59	203	340
39	Asia	Burma	Irrawaddy	.430	100	616	619
40	Asia	Bangladesh	Ganges/Brahm	1.480	66	1,128	1,720

Table 3-1

ANNUAL WATER AND SEDIMENT YIELD OF WORLD'S RIVERS
AT OCEAN LEVEL - cont'd...

No	Continent	Country/ Economy	River	D. Area (mill km^2)	Runoff (cm)	Sediment (t/km^2)	Yield (ppm)
41	Asia	India	Mehandi	.130	52	15	30
42	Asia	India	Damodar	.020	50	1,400	2,800
43	Asia	India	Godavari	.310	27	310	1,143
44	Asia	Pakistan	Indus	.970	25	454	1,849
45	Asia	Iraq	Tigris-Eupha	1.050	4	50	1,152
46	Africa	Egypt	Nile	2.960	1	38	3,700
47	Africa	Nigeria	Niger	1.210	16	33	208
48	Africa	Zaire	Zaire	3.820	33	11	34
49	Africa	S. Africa	Orange	1.020	1	17	1,545
50	Africa	Mozambique	Zambesi	1.200	19	17	90
51	Africa	Mozambique	Limpopo	.410	1	80	6,600
52	Africa	Tanzania	Rufiji	.180	5	94	1,889
53	Oceania	Australia	Murray	1.060	2	28	1,364
54	Oceania	New Zealand	Haast	.001	600	13,000	2,167
55	Oceania	New Guinea	Fly	.061	126	492	390
56	Oceania	New Guinea	Purari	.031	248	2,581	1,039
57	Oceania	Taiwan	Choshui	.003	200	22,000	11,000
58	Oceania	Taiwan	Kaoping	.003	300	13,000	4,333
59	Oceania	Taiwan	Tsengwen	.001	200	28,000	14,000
60	Oceania	Taiwan	Hualien	.002	200	9,500	4,750

Table 3-1

ANNUAL WATER AND SEDIMENT YIELD OF WORLD'S RIVERS
AT OCEAN LEVEL - cont'd...

No.	Continent	Country/ Economy	River	D. Area (mill km^2)	Runoff (cm)	Sediment (t/km^2)	Yield (ppm)
61	Oceania	Taiwan	Peinan	.002	200	9,500	4,750
62	Oceania	Taiwan	Hsiukuluan	.002	200	8,000	4,000

Notes:

1. Data based on Milliman and Meade (1983).
2. For Colorado, Mississippi, Indus and Nile rivers, sediment data are based on Holeman (1968) to reflect pre-dam condition. Sediment yields (tons/km^2/yr) are:

	Colorado	Mississ.	Indus	Nile
Holeman (1968):	210.9	106.7	453.6	37.5
Milliman & Meade (1983):	0.2	64.2	103.1	0.0

For comparative purposes, the top 20 basins ranked by drainage area, unit runoff, sediment yield and sediment concentration are listed in Tables 3-2 thru 3-5, respectively. In the ranking tables, minor basins with areas less than 10,000 km^2 have been excluded.

World-wide data on precipitation, unit runoff and sediment yield for various geographic regions are summarized in Table 3-6. Water data in this table are based on Table 11 of UNESCO (1977), and the sediment data on Milliman and Meade (1983).

In viewing the sediment data in the above tables, it should be noted that they are based on measured suspended loads near ocean level and that about 15 percent should be added to these figures to account for the unmeasured load and measurements missed during rare events. Further, the data in Table 3-6 should be viewed as indicative of world-wide distribution of relevant hydrologic parameters and not as definitive information. In the original sources, used herein, extensive extrapolations have been made due to sparseness of information and slightly different definitions of geographic regions have been used in the runoff and sediment load data.

The above data show:

1. The largest amount of meteoric precipitation and runoff occurs in South America, followed by Asia. However, the sediment erosion rates in Asia are about four times larger. In fact, Asia's sediment yield is more than twice of the world average.

2. The largest sediment yields occur in Oceania. For the smaller basins in New Zealand, New Guinea and Taiwan, sediment yields are 2-3 orders of magnitude larger than the world average.

3. The world-wide average yield is around 165 t/km^2/yr. With additional 15 percent, see footnote 4 of Table 2, this would

Table 3-2

ANNUAL WATER AND SEDIMENT YIELD OF WORLD'S RIVERS
BY DRAINAGE AREA

No	Continent	Country/ Economy	River	D. Area (mill km^2)	Runoff (cm)	Sediment (t/km^2)	Yield (ppm)
1	S. America	Brazil	Amazon	6.150	102	146	143
2	Africa	Zaire	Zaire	3.820	33	11	34
3	N. America	USA	Mississippi	3.270	18	107	602
4	Africa	Egypt	Nile	2.960	1	38	3,700
5	S. America	Argentina	La Plata	2.830	17	33	196
6	Eu. Arctic	USSR	Yenisei	2.580	22	5	23
7	Eu. Arctic	USSR	Lena	2.500	21	5	23
8	Eu. Arctic	USSR	Ob	2.500	15	6	42
9	Asia	China	Yangtze	1.940	46	246	531
10	Asia	USSR	Amur	1.850	18	28	160
11	N. America	Canada	Mackenzie	1.810	17	55	327
12	Asia	Bangladesh	Ganges/Brahm	1.480	66	1,128	1,720
13	Africa	Nigeria	Niger	1.210	16	33	208
14	Africa	Mozambique	Zambesi	1.200	19	17	90
15	Oceania	Australia	Murray	1.060	2	28	1,364
16	Asia	Iraq	Tigris-Eupha	1.050	4	50	1,152
17	N. America	Canada	St. Lawrence	1.030	43	4	9
18	Africa	S. Africa	Orange	1.020	1	17	1,545
19	S. America	Venezuela	Orinoco	.990	111	212	191
20	Asia	Pakistan	Indus	.970	25	454	1,849

See foot notes under Table 3-1.

Table 3-3

ANNUAL WATER AND SEDIMENT YIELD OF WORLD'S RIVERS
BY UNIT RUNOFF

No	Continent	Country/ Economy	River	D. Area (mill km²)	Runoff (cm)	Sediment (t/km²)	Yield (ppm)
1	Oceania	New Guinea	Purari	.031	248	2,581	1,039
2	Oceania	New Guinea	Fly	.061	126	492	390
3	S. America	Venezuela	Orinoco	.990	111	212	191
4	Asia	Viet Nam	Hungho	.120	103	1,083	1,057
5	S. America	Brazil	Amazon	6.150	102	146	143
6	Asia	Burma	Irrawaddy	.430	100	616	619
7	S. America	Colombia	Magdelena	.240	99	917	928
8	N. America	USA	Susitna	.050	80	500	625
9	Asia	China	Pearl	.440	69	157	228
10	Europe	Italy	Po	.070	66	214	326
11	Asia	Bangladesh	Ganges/Brahm	1.480	66	1,128	1,720
12	N. America	USA	Copper	.060	65	1,167	1,795
13	N. America	USA	Hudson	.020	60	50	83
14	Asia	Viet Nam	Mekong	.790	59	203	340
15	Europe	France	Rhone	.090	54	111	204
16	Asia	India	Mehandi	.130	52	15	30
17	N. America	Canada	Fraser	.220	51	91	179
18	Asia	India	Damodar	.020	50	1,400	2,800
19	Asia	China	Yangtze	1.940	46	246	531
20	N. America	Canada	St. Lawrence	1.030	43	4	9

See foot notes under Table 3-1.

Table 3-4

ANNUAL WATER AND SEDIMENT YIELD OF WORLD'S RIVERS,
BY SEDIMENT YIELD

No	Continent	Country/ Economy	River	D. Area (mill km^2)	Runoff (cm)	Sediment Yield (t/km^2)	(ppm)
1	Oceania	New Guinea	Purari	.031	248	2,581	1,039
2	S. America	Peru	Chira	.020	25	2,000	8,000
3	Asia	China	Daling	.020	5	1,800	36,000
4	Asia	China	Haiho	.050	4	1,620	40,500
5	Asia	China	Yellow	.770	6	1,403	22,041
6	Asia	India	Damodar	.020	50	1,400	2,800
7	N. America	USA	Copper	.060	65	1,167	1,795
8	Asia	Bangladesh	Ganges/Brahm	1.480	66	1,128	1,720
9	Asia	Vietnam	Hungho	.120	103	1,083	1,057
10	S. America	Colombia	Magdelena	.240	99	917	928
11	Asia	Burma	Irrawaddy	.430	100	616	619
12	N. America	USA	Susitna	.050	80	500	625
13	Oceania	New Guinea	Fly	.061	126	492	390
14	Asia	Pakistan	Indus	.970	25	454	1,849
15	Asia	India	Godavari	.310	27	310	1,143
16	Asia	China	Yangtze	1.940	46	246	531
17	Asia	China	Liaohe	.170	4	241	6,833
18	Europe	Italy	Po	.070	66	214	326
19	S. America	Venezuela	Orinoco	.990	111	212	191
20	N. America	Mexico	Colorado	.640	3	211	6,750

See foot notes under Table 3-1.

Table 3-5

ANNUAL WATER AND SEDIMENT YIELD OF WORLD'S RIVERS, BY SEDIMENT YIELD

No	Continent	Country/ Economy	River	D. Area (mill km²)	Runoff (cm)	Sediment (t/km²)	Yield (ppm)
1	Asia	China	Haiho	.050	4	1,620	40,500
2	Asia	China	Daling	.020	5	1,800	36,000
3	Asia	China	Yellow	.770	6	1,403	22,041
4	S. America	Peru	Chira	.020	25	2,000	8,000
5	Asia	China	Liaohe	.170	4	241	6,833
6	N. America	Mexico	Colorado	.640	3	211	6,750
7	Africa	Mozambique	Limpopo	.410	1	80	6,600
8	Africa	Egypt	Nile	2.960	1	38	3,700
9	Asia	India	Damodar	.020	50	1,400	2,800
10	N. America	USA	Brazos	.110	6	145	2,286
11	Africa	Tanzania	Rufiji	.180	5	94	1,889
12	Asia	Pakistan	Indus	.970	25	454	1,849
13	N. America	USA	Copper	.060	65	1,167	1,795
14	Asia	Bangladesh	Ganges/Brahm	1.480	66	1,128	1,720
15	Africa	S. Africa	Orange	1.020	1	17	1,545
16	Oceania	Australia	Murray	1.060	2	28	1,364
17	Asia	Iraq	Tigris-Eupha	1.050	4	50	1,152
18	Asia	India	Godavari	.310	27	310	1,143
19	Asia	Viet Nam	Hungho	.120	103	1,083	1,057
20	Oceania	New Guinea	Purari	.031	248	2,581	1,039

See foot notes under Table 3-1.

Table 3-6

WORLD DISTRIBUTION OF RUNOFF AND SEDIMENT LOAD

Geographic Area	Precipitation			Runoff		Measured Suspended Sediment		Load
	mm	km^3	%	km^3	%	billion tons/yr	%	yield (t/km^2/yr)
(1)	(2)	(3)	(4)	(5)	(6)	(7)	(8)	(9)
North America	756	15.8	15.4	6.6	17.1	1.46	10.9	84
Asia	740	25.7	25.0	10.8	28.0	6.35	47.4	380
Africa	740	19.7	19.2	4.2	10.9	0.53	3.9	35
South America	1,600	27.0	26.2	11.8	30.5	1.79	13.3	97
Europe	790	7.5	7.3	2.7	7.0	0.23	1.7	50
Australia	791	7.1	6.9	2.5	6.5	0.06	0.4	28
Oceania						3.00	22.4	1,000
TOTAL	–	102.8	100.0	38.6	100.0	13.42	100.0	165

Notes: 1. Above data should be viewed as indicative rather than definitive, mainly because of extrapolations necessitated in original sources. Also, slightly different definitions of geographic areas have been used in the runoff and sediment data.
2. Precipitation and Runoff data, Columns (2) – (6) based on UNESCO (1977), Table 11. Runoff includes groundwater not drained by rivers.
3. Sediment data, Columns (7) – (9) based on Milliman and Meade (1983), Table 4. Their data on Eurasian Arctic has been excluded from average field.
4. Sediment data pertain to measured suspended load at mouth of basins, near ocean level. To these, add about 10 percent for unmeasured suspended and bedload and another 5 percent for unmeasured load during catastrophic events.

amount to about 190 t/km^2/yr. The average sediment yield for the measured rivers is 148 t/km^2/yr and it corresponds to a concentration of 425 ppm. With the additional 15 percent, the measured concentration would be 490 ppm.

4. Of the measured parameters, sediment yield is most correlated with drainage area (Fig. 3-1) The best-fit trendline between sediment yield and drainage area would indicate a value of b in Eq. (3.1) of around 0.8. Notwithstanding the different climatic, pedologic, tectonic and land use conditions between different basins, the sediment yield does appear to strongly decline for larger basins.

5. Sediment concentration is inversely correlated with the unit runoff. If unit runoff is looked at as an indicator of the excess of precipitation over actual evapotranspiration, then a small unit runoff would indicate aridity and, hence, poor vegetal cover. For basins larger than 20,000 km^2, eight largest concentrations (1,890 - 40,500 ppm) are associated with runoff of 6 cm or less.

Human Impact on Sediment Yield

Within the zonal distributions mentioned above, human actions have made their impact on sediment yield. Over the last century or two, a great deal of world's forests have been cleared for agricultural and urbanization needs. Agricultural activity along with strip mining and other large construction projects, increases the on-site erodibility of soil by loosening it and destroying its protective layer. Studies in the U.S. show that conversion of forest land to row cropping can increase on-site erosion by a factor of 100-1,000 and from pasture land to construction of about 200 (Mahmood, 1977).

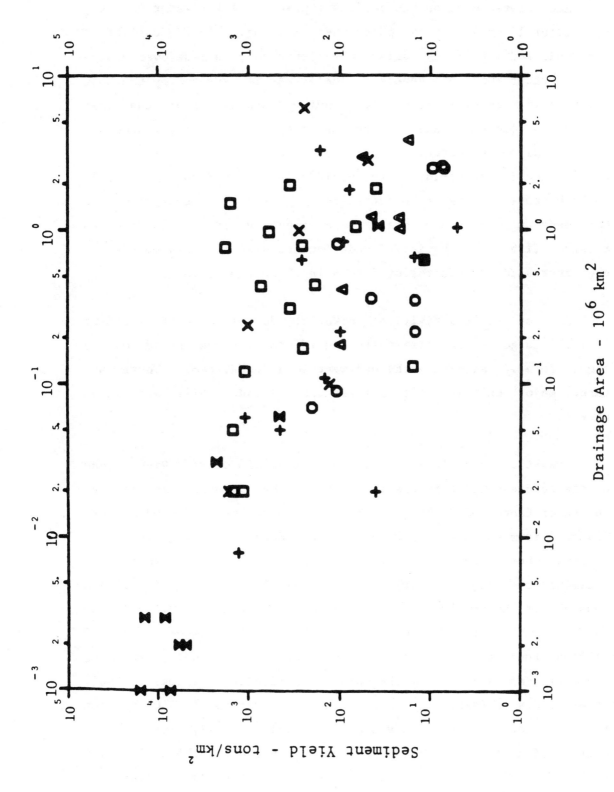

FIG. 3-1 SEDIMENT YIELD VERSUS DRAINAGE AREA OF WORLD
RIVER (Measured Suspended Load)

Accelerated erosion has serious implications for water quality; agricultural productivity and channel flooding. In the context of reservoir sedimentation, unless the disturbance is made over large areas, their impact is generally small. As illustrated by the Coon Creek basin, referred to earlier, sediment storage within the basin results in long time lags between the inception of a disturbance and the arrival of its effect at the mouth of basin. Two major areas of disturbance in the world are the plain's region of Europe and U.S.A. In both cases, large scale conversion of forest land to agriculture has made a measurable impact on sediment yield. According to Strakhov (1967), mechanical denudation measured at basin mouths has been increased by a factor of 3 to 5 in these two regions.

All of man's activities, however, do not increase sediment yield. Large storage reservoirs significantly decrease and, many a time, totally eliminate the sediment load downstream. There are three major examples of this effect on Colorado, Nile and Indus Rivers.

Dramatic reduction in the sediment load of Colorado River - one of the muddiest major rivers in the U.S., has occurred as a consequence of Hoover Dam. This has been documented by Meade and Parker, (1985), from the analysis of suspended sediment discharge at Yuma, Arizona where the river leaves the U.S. According to them, the sediment discharge in this river has declined from 135 million tons/yr of Holeman's estimate to its current value of 0.1 million tons/yr. Similarly, River Nile, that used to transport about 110 million tons/yr of sediment at its delta, is virtually free of sediment, as a result of the completion of High Aswan Dam in 1964. River Indus in Pakistan, which used to deliver about 440 million tons/yr, now delivers only about 100 million tons/yr due to the construction of: two major dams (Mangla, 1965 and Tarbela, 1974), a number of low diversion dams (barrages) and an increased transfer of water and sediment into the irrigation canal system.

28

The case of Missouri-Mississippi river system is even more illustrative. In this case, the construction of six major dams in the Missouri basin (Gavins Point, the most downstream one, completed in 1953), coupled with extensive channel stabilization along the whole river, mainly for navigation and flood control purposes, has reduced the sediment discharge to the Gulf of Mexico to one-half of what it was in 1953. The contribution of channel bank erosion to sediment yield can be rather large. In Sacramento River, California, 60 percent of the total sediment inflow of 12.7 million tons/year has been estimated to come from streambank erosion (Sing, 1986). The effect of channel stabilization is that the valley deposit which can be reworked by the nascent river are no more available as a sediment source.

Impact of Natural Events

Sediment production from a basin is a discontinuous process. It is usually associated with rainfall events. Floods, earthquakes, volcanos and mudflows are some of the other events that cause unusually large amounts of sediment production. In recent times, all of these have been documented in various parts of the world.

New Madrid Earthquake: Between December, 1811 and February, 1812, the greatest earthquake in the continental U.S was experienced near New Madrid in South Missouri. There were three major shocks and many aftershocks. The one in 1874 was large enough to be felt as far away as 500 km. The area of greatest shaking was about 100,000 km^2. Large scale bank caving and fissuring introduced an undetermined, but major quantities of sediment in Mississippi. Both Winkely (1977) and Walters (1975) believe that, as a result of New Madrid Earthquake, the sediment loading of Mississippi was significantly increased, and the channel morphology was changed because of that.

Kosi River Mudflow: Sapt Kosi is the third largest river emanating from the Himalayan Range. It is exceeded in size only by Indus and Brahamaputra Rivers. Kosi watershed extends across the Himalayan range into the Tibetan Plateau and it has the distinction of draining Mount Everest, Kinchunchunga and Makato. This river has three main tributaries, Sun Kosi, Arun and Tamur. Arun, which draws about 58 percent of the catchment extends northward into the Tibet Plateau. Precipitation in Kosi watershed comprises both rainfall (89%) and snowfall (11%). About 80-85 percent of total annual rainfall occurs during monsoon months of June - August. Between June and September, the runoff amounts to 85 percent and the sediment load about 98 percent of the annual value (Mahmood, 1981).

Regular stream gaging and rainfall measurements on Kosi were started in 1947 and 1948, respectively, at Barahkshtra in the foothills. Details of sediment sampling procedures used in Kosi gaging are not documented. The writer's investigation in 1979 revealed that up to a discharge of 15,000 m^3/s, a single suspended load sample was obtained at 0.6 times the flow depth below the water surface, and at higher stages dip samples from the surface were being used. At the gaging site, the river is a confined channel with steep gradient and high velocities. Under these conditions, most of the sand size load will be uniformly distributed in the channel depth, but some underestimation of sediment load is likely.

Himalayas are geologically young and abound in seismic activity. It is estimated (Chaudhry, H.M, 1973) that about two percent of the total annual global energy release takes place in the Himalayan region. Two of the world's worst earthquakes, in terms of lives lost, occurred in Assam in 1897 and 1950, not far from the Kosi catchment. Kathmandu earthquake of 1934, which levelled most of the city was reportedly centered 120 km off Barahkhstra gaging site.

At the gaging site, Kosi has a drainage area of 59,000 km^2 with an average annual runoff of 53,000 Mm^3. The average annual sediment yield based on measured suspended sediment is about 2,800 t/km^2 of which about 16 percent is coarse sand; 29 percent medium sand and 55 percent is silt and clay. The average annual measured concentration is 3,110 ppm.

On the night of June 23-24, 1980, after three days of heavy rainfall, a major landslide occurred in the catchment of Tamur, the eastern tributary. The slide blocked Yangma Khola, a tributary of Tamur. The blockage was naturally breached in the early hours of June 24 and the impounded water and sediment were released in Tamur. About 130 kms downstream of the original slide, the first effect of the event was noticed at about mid-day. In two hours the water level rose by 3.6 m and the flow carried (Revio, 1980) "... huge quantities of debris, logs, animal carcasses and about four bodies..." By about 15:15, the water level dropped by 1.5 m and debris was almost completely absent. Between 15:30 and 15:45, the level rose again, but this time, the flow seemed to be of a viscous fluid. The surface was greasy smooth with loud rumbling and grinding noise. Boulders, as large as 150 tons were moving in the shallow side of the channel section rather easily. Samples taken at this stage showed a sediment content of 80 percent by volume with particle sizes 10 mm and under with 23 percent lying below 0.075 mm. The solids were non-plastic, with a specific gravity of 2.68 and a liquid limit of 17.5%. The velocity of flow was 10 m/sec during the initial rise and 6-7 m/sec during the flood flow. The writer flew over the effected catchment and Kosi River channel during October 1980. From aerial and field inspections of deposits, he estimated that the mudflow transported between 55-65 million tons of sediment over a period of about 14 hours. This is equivalent to 36 percent of the annual load or five times the average monthly load for the month of June.

31

Eruption of Mount St. Helens: Mount St. Helens in Southwestern Washington, erupted on May 18, 1980. As a result, mudflows developed in the main drainage channels. (Cummans, 1981). It has been estimated that following the eruption, a massive debris avalanche deposited about a billion tons of rock, ice and other materials in the upper 17 miles of the North Fork Toutle River Valley. Following the avalanche, a mudflow developed which deposited about 50 million tons of sediment in Cowlitz River channel. It has been estimated (Meade and Parker, 1985) that in the first four months after eruption, about 140 million tons of suspended sediment were deposited by the Cowlitz River into the Columbia River. In the last few years, this has diminished to about 30 million tons/year. As a result of Mount St. Helen's eruption, the sediment yield of Columbia River has currently increased to 40 million tons/year from the pre-eruption value of 10 million tons/yr.

Sediment load in rivers, generally increases as a power function of discharge. Disproportionately larger quantities of sediment are, therefore, transported during high flow than the low flows. Meade and Parker (1985) estimate that in the coterminous United States, about one-half of the annual sediment load is transported during 5-10 days flow. Flood flows are also caused by hurricanes, and the above named authors estimate that hurricane induced floods in Juniata, Delaware and Eel rivers transported 3-10 years of average sediment load in a matter of 10 days. Schumm (1977) cites accelerated denudation in New Guinea where the earthquakes of 1970 triggered debris avalanches that denuded slopes over 60 km^2 and resulted in an almost instantaneous denudation of 11.5 cm compared to the regional normal rate of 20 cm/1000 yrs.

Measurement of Sediment Load

As shown above, a great deal is understood about the weathering, erosion and transport processes that contribute to the sediment load in river basins. Regional average information and short-term average sediment yields are usually available in major basins. However, they are not adequate for the sedimentation design of storage reservoirs. Sediment loads contributed by infrequent events alone are sufficient to undo many estimates based on short-term data. The writer was actively involved in the design of remedial sediment control works for Chattra Main Canal offtaking from Kosi River in Nepal. The design was at a fairly advanced stage when the mudflow of June, 1980 occurred. In addition to the problem of sudden, extreme sediment load, the mudflow caused a major change in the alignment and bed level of the river channel. As a result, a substantial revision of designs became necessary and was carried out. The mudflow in Kosi had not been anticipated and the previous 10 years of sediment data had no record of similar events.

It is customary and necessary to measure sediment loads at or near the proposed sites of storage reservoirs. Sediment measurements are made in conjunction with water discharge measurements. Standard practice for these measurement has been outlined in various U.S. Geological Survey Publications. Guy (1969, 1970) and Guy and Norman (1970) present a useful summary of basic sedimentation concepts, measurement procedures and laboratory methods needed for sediment load measurements in rivers. Site data for sediment load are invaluable. Ideally, one would like to have data for a period, at least, equal to about one-half the project life. However, except in fairly developed water resources systems, or in special cases where the project formulation has dragged on for decades, such data are not available. In these circumstances, one has to be content to use whatever data and ancillary information can be collected. It is rare that a project implementation has been voided for lack of

adequate sediment load data.   In all cases and, especially, when
sediment load records are inadequate, specialist help in the interpretation of data and estimation of long-term average sediment loads
is invaluable.

Special Considerations

Some general principles can be formulated about the collection
and analysis of sediment load data for reservoir design. Hydrologic
series in arid and semi-arid climates show larger variability than
in the humid climates. Given similar circumstances, a longer
sediment load data base will be required in the former climates.
Experience with the sediment load transported by floods indicates
that, in case of limited resources, it is better to carry out more
frequent measurements during high flows than the low flows. Efforts
should be made to measure the extreme flow events, if one is lucky
enough to experience them before the construction stage.

Anthropogenic changes and natural events in a basin can alter
past trends. In large basins, man's actions will usually have
relatively milder impact on reservoir sedimentation than the natural
events.   In the sedimentation design of storage reservoirs,
contributions from earthquakes, volcanos, mudflows and hurricanes
are especially relevant and should be investigated. Generally, the
seismic activity at the project site is studied for other design
considerations, such as the stability of embankment and foundation
and, hurricanes are investigated in the estimation of design floods.
The sediment production by mudflows is not normally included in the
design studies and is likely to be ignored. This should be given
special attention. Techniques, such as geomorphic analysis of
drainage basins, should be used to define the extent and magnitude
of hillslope instability and to check estimates derived from gaging
data.

CHAPTER IV

RESERVOIR SEDIMENTATION PROCESSES

Sediment load carried by a flow will drop out if the transport capacity of flow is diminished. In general, the capacity of a given flow decreases with a reduction of its velocity. As a river enters the reservoir, the cross-sectional area of flow is increased, the average velocity is decreased and sediment load starts dropping out. The order in which different sediment sizes settle down and the location of deposits depends on three physical phenomena--cessation of drag force on particles rolling along the stream bed (bedload); reduction in turbulence level which determines the capacity of flow to maintain sediment suspension and, development of density currents. In all of these, the physical size of sediment particle plays an important role. Once the sediment particles have settled out of flow, they assume a certain initial density which is also a function, of particle size. The density of deposits is an important variable because a given mass of sediment will occupy a larger share of the storage volume if its density is low. This chapter presents basic information about the properties of sediment, entrainment and transport of sediment by flow and the processes of deposition in storage reservoirs.

Sediment Size

The range of particle sizes found in nature is rather large--fraction of a micron for clay to large boulders a few meters across. From the viewpoint of reservoir sedimentation, however, the range of interest varies from clay to gravel as the mass rate of transport associated with larger particles is insignificant.

The following descriptive names are used to classify different size fractions of sediments:

Gravel: 64 mm   –   2   mm
Sand: 2 mm   –   62   microns
Silt: 62 microns –   4   microns
Clay: 4 microns –   0.24 microns

This nomenclature was initially adopted by American Geophysical Union in 1947 and is accepted as a standard terminology in sedimentation engineering. Further sub-classes, each covering a two-fold range of size, have also been established within the above and they are based on adjectives, such as, coarse, medium or fine. In some parts of the world, slightly different size ranges have been conventionally used, especially to describe the sub-classes. For example, the lower size limit for sand may be given as 75 microns, and that for clay as 5.5 microns. This discrepancy is not overly critical in the interpretation of sediment load data, provided the distribution of total load amongst all the classes is available.

It is difficult to describe the size of a sediment particle by a single linear dimension due to variations of its shape. Various "sizes" have been used in sedimentation engineering and its allied disciplines. However, in sedimentation engineering, two sizes are most commonly used: sieve size, which is the side length of smallest square sieve opening through which the particle will pass, and fall diameter, which is the diameter of a sphere with a specific gravity of 2.65 that will have the same terminal fall velocity in quiescent water at 24°C as the original particle. Sieve diameters are more commonly used for sand and gravel, mainly because of the wide-spread use of sieving in size analysis. The fall diameter can be looked at as a hydraulic behavioral size, for it represents the combined effect of a number of variables, such as, specific gravity, size, shape and texture of particle. In suspended mode of sediment transport, the behavioral size is more relevant, and empirical curves have been developed to translate the sieve diameter of water borne sediments to fall diameter for given shape factors (Federal Inter-Agency Sedimentation Project, 1957).

The fall velocity of a sediment particle is, generally, described in terms of its terminal value when falling in quiescent water. Although direct measurements have not been made, it is generally agreed on the basis of theoretical considerations and some indirect evidence that the fall velocity of a given sediment particle will be smaller in turbulent fluids than in quiescent ones. In the case of a spherical particle, the terminal fall velocity can be determined by equating the gravitational force with the fluid drag to yield

$$w = 4/3 \cdot [(S_g - 1)gD]^{\frac{1}{2}}/C_D \qquad (4.1)$$

where, w = fall velocity, S_g = specific gravity, g = gravitational acceleration, D = diameter and C_D, the drag coefficient is a function of fall velocity Reynold Number

$$C_D = f[R] \qquad (4.2)$$

$$R = wD/\nu \qquad (4.3)$$

where, ν = kinematic viscosity of the fluid and function $f[.]$ has to be empirically determined. Only when $R < 0.1$ (D roughly less than 50 microns), theoretical value of C_D is

$$C_D = 24/R \cdot \qquad (4.4)$$

The fall velocity decreases with particle size, but in the sand to clay size range, it decreases at a much faster rate than Eq. (4.1) would indicate. For example, when the particle size reduces by one-fiftieth from 250 to 5 microns, the fall velocity reduces by 1/500, mainly due to the increase in C_D. For practical computations, Eq. (4.4) can be applied to the silt and clay size range. For sands, curves developed by Federal Inter-Agency Sedimentation Project (1957) are available. However, the following empirical equation developed by Rubey (1933) will also yield acceptable values.

$$w = \frac{\sqrt{\frac{2}{3} g(S_g - 1)D^3 + 36\, \nu^2} - 6\nu}{D} \, . \tag{4.5}$$

All of the variables in Rubey's Equation should be expressed in consistent units. The writer likes to express the fall velocity in terms of parametric time, T_*, which is time in seconds taken by a sediment particle to fall through its own diameter. The variation of T_* with sediment particle size over a range of 0.1 to 1000 microns is shown in Fig. 4-1. In the very fine-to-coarse sand range, the value of T_* is around 0.008 sec. For 1 micron clay particle, T_* is slightly more than 1 sec.

Entrainment

In smooth boundary flows, the frictional drag emanates from the shear stress exerted on the solid boundary. In alluvial channel flows with bed forms, part of the drag comes from the shear force and the remainder from pressure drag on the bed forms. The shear force is transmitted to individual particles which start to move if the force is large enough to overcome their frictional resistance. The movement of individual grains on the bed is not continuous. It is punctuated by rest periods and the average rate of travel of particles is much slower than the velocity of flow. As the flow rate and the boundary shear stress increase further, the sediment particles are lifted into the flow where they are supported by the vertical component of turbulence and they move at the velocity of surrounding fluid. Flow condition when the particles just start to

38

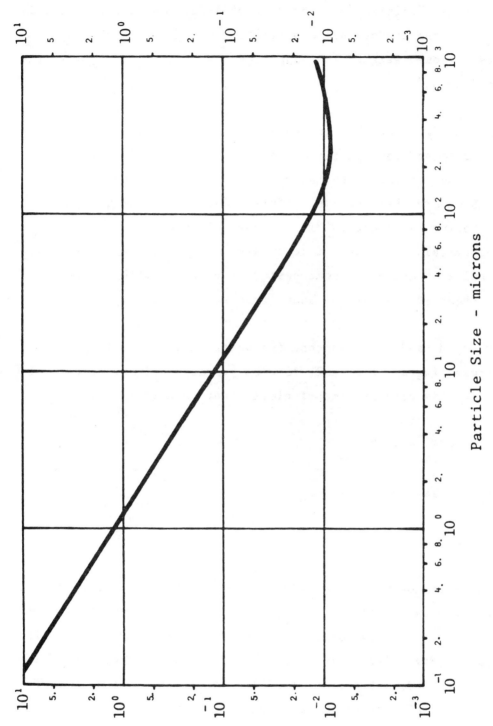

Particle Size - microns

Time to Settle through Diameter, T_*, sec

FIG. 4-1 FALL PROPERTIES OF SEDIMENT IN QUIESCENT WATER (Unhindered Settlement at 40° C)

39

move is termed "critical". Movement of particles that are mainly supported by the channel bed constitutes "bedload" and that of the particles whose weight is supported by turbulence forms the "suspended load."

In accordance with the above concept of flow drag being transmitted to sediment particles in the channel bed, critical flow condition for sediment entrainment is defined in terms of the average boundary shear stress. This model is basically applicable to noncohesive sediments. In the case of cohesive sediment the electro-chemical bonding forces are more complex than the intergranular friction of noncohesive materials and the concept of critical shear stress has not been found to be valid.

For sand and other noncohesive particles, Shield's critical shear stress diagram, Fig. 4-2, is widely accepted in practice. The ordinate in this case is dimensionless shear parameter

$$\tau_* = \tau_o / [\gamma (S_g - 1) D] \tag{4.6}$$

and, the abscissa is

$$R_* = U_* D / \nu \tag{4.7}$$

where, τ_o = boundary shear stress given by $\gamma\, dS$, γ = unit weight of water, S = energy gradient of flow, d = depth of flow and U_* = shear velocity, $\sqrt{\tau_o / \rho}$. Flow conditions represented by points below the line shown in Fig. 4-2, imply no entrainment while those above the line mean that sediment particles will be entrained by the flow. For values of $R_* = 500$, or so, τ_* assumes a constant value of 0.06. In this range,

$$\tau_o = 0.296\, D \tag{4.8}$$

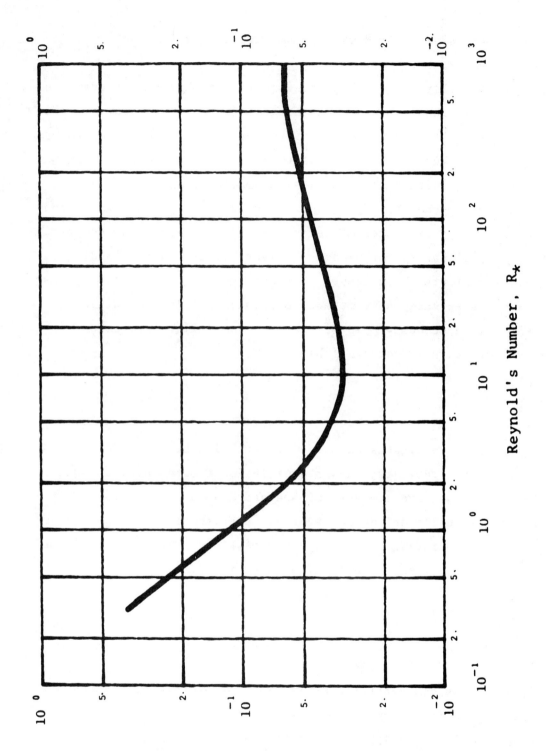

Reynold's Number, R_*

Dimensionless Shear Stress, τ_*

FIG. 4-2 SHIELD'S CRITICAL SHEAR STRESS DIAGRAM

41

where, τ_o is expressed in N/m^2, D in mm and $S_g = 2.65$.

Conventionally, the shear stress used in Shield's diagram is the average bed shear stress. Measurement of boundary shear stress on the bed of sand bed canals with ripple and dune bed forms (Mahmood and Haque, 1985), shows that due to the pressure drag on bed forms, the average shear stress is smaller than the value of τ_o given above and that it experiences considerable spatial variation related to the existence of secondary flow cells and temporal variations related to turbulence. Nevertheless, Shield's diagram has been validated by a number of other investigators and it is recognized as an acceptable method to predict critical condition for movement of noncohesive bed sediments. A similar criterion for cohesive materials is not available.

Suspension

There is a continuous exchange of particles between bedload and suspended load. However, under equilibrium flow conditions, where stable time and space averages of bedload and suspended load exist, it is possible to define an average distribution of suspended sediment concentration along the depth of flow. The concentration profile most widely accepted in literature is given by

$$\frac{C_y}{C_a} = \left[\left(\frac{d-y}{y}\right) \left(\frac{a}{d-a}\right) \right]^z \qquad (4.9)$$

where, C_y = mass concentration of sediment at a distance y above the channel bed, C_a = concentration at a reference distance y = a, z = $w/(\kappa U_*)$, and, κ von Karman's constant = 0.4. According to this equation, the concentration of suspended sediment decreases from near the channel bed towards the free surface. The form of Eq. (4.9) has been extensively verified on laboratory flumes as well as sand bed canal and river data. Measured values of exponent z, however, show considerable variation from the theoretical value given above. This exponent plays an important role in determining the nonuniformity of concentration profile and the mass of sediment carried in suspension. If the value of z is greater than about 5, there will be almost no suspended load and if it is less than 0.1, the sediment profile will have a nearly uniform distribution.

Fine Material Load

In sediment transport theory, the load that consists of particle sizes found in the bed material is called the bed material load. Often, the sediment load will contain a large proportion of particles which are not significantly represented in the bed material. This part of the load is called wash load. In sand bed channels, the wash load, generally, comprises of particle in silt and clay size range, so that the cutoff size for wash load is 62.5 microns. For this reason, the silt and clay load in such channels is called the fine material load. The bed material load can be theoretically calculated, within acceptable degree of accuracy, from the local hydraulic conditions and bed material composition. The wash load cannot be so calculated. Its value can only be determined by actual measurement.

The quantity of fine material load in a flow depends on its generation within the drainage basin including its supply from sediment sources such as slope and bank erosion. The proportion of fine material load in total sediment load carried by a flow varies with the flow discharge and the order of flow in the yearly sequence of high discharges. In general, the first flood of the season will produce the highest amount of fine material load. On an annual basis, most sand bed rivers carry more fine material than sand load. The proportion of different size fractions in some typical rivers is given below.

River	Percent of Annual Sediment Load			
	Sand	Silt	Clay	Silt+Clay
Nile at Old Aswan Dam	30	40	30	70
Missouri at Omaha (pre-dams)	20	–	–	80
Mississippi at Vicksburg (1973-74)	32	–	–	68
Indus at Tarbela	59	34	7	41
Indus at Kalabagh	38	51	11	62
Kabul at Warsak (pre-dam)	12	60	28	88
Kosi at Barahkhstra	45	–	–	55

The suspended sediment samplers used in the measurement of suspended load, on which the above data are based, stop about 7.5-10 cm short of the actual bed and bedload is not included in the reported data. The actual proportion of sand in the above data will, therefore, be slightly higher. Nevertheless, the high proportion of fine material load in rivers, which cannot be predicted from sediment transport theories, makes it imperative that sediment load at a storage site be actually measured. Also, it calls for caution in applying sediment transport theories pertaining to channel flow, to reservoir sedimentation problems. The importance of fine material load in channel flows is relatively small, except in an indirect manner relating to channel morphology. In storage reservoirs, on the other hand, the fine material load forms roughly half the load and as shown later, it occupies more storage space per unit mass than the sand fraction.

Bed Material Load

A number of equations to predict bedload are available in sediment literature. Direct measurement of bedload in sand bed flows is nearly impossible and in general, the predictive equations can only be tested in the context of bed material load. Bedload and bed material load equations available in literature differ in their theoretical content. Verifications of sediment transport equations on prototype data (Mahmood et al, 1979. and Mahmood, 1980) conclude that whereas Einstein's Bedload Function is the most profound, Toffaleti's method is most accurate when tested against Missouri River and Pakistan's ACOP canal data.

A package of computer programs to calculate bed material load in sand bed and gravel channels by various transport functions is available (Mahmood, 1982 and 1983). However, in view of the implicit nature of most bedload equations, a simplified empirical form is sometimes used.

$$g_b = a \, [\quad _o]^b$$

where, g_b = bedload in units of mass per unit time per unit width and b = constant over a narrow range. Values of b vary from about 4.0 at the commencement of entrainment to about 1.5 at higher rates of transport.

Unit Weight of Deposits

When sediment is first deposited in a reservoir, its density is determined by the mode of deposition, its particle size distribution and the chemical regime of water. Later on, as the deposits are loaded with additional deposits, the silts and clays are compacted to higher densities. The unit weight of deposit at a given time is a function of: weight of overburden; particle size distribution; degree of exposure to drying; permeability and the elapsed time since first deposit. The exposure to drying is most important for clays whose density may as much as double in a matter of few months exposure. Direct measurement of in-situ density of deposits is difficult due to the disturbance caused by usual geotechnical

45

sampling methods. Density measurements can be made by Gamma Probe (McHenry et al, 1965, 1971; U.S. Army Corps of Engineers, 1965). Many a time, the values reported in literature have been indirectly obtained by using the measured volume of deposits and sediment load inflow.

A method for predicting the unit weight of reservoir deposits is given by Lane and Koelzer (1943). This is based on indirect measurements and is most commonly used in practice. In this method, the dry density of deposits W_t at a given age of T years is

$$W_t = W_1 + B \log(T) . \hspace{3cm} (4.11)$$

Variables W_1, the unit weight at the end of first year, and B are expressed in terms of particle size classification, and the exposure environment of deposits. The latter is, of necessity, qualitative and it is specified in four classes as: always or nearly submerged; exposed by moderate drawdown; exposed by considerable drawdown, and exposed by a normally empty reservoir. The variation of W_t, based on the above method, for sand, silt and clay size fractions is graphically presented in Fig. 4-3. It is noted that the density for sand is independent of age and exposure environment and that for clay is most sensitive to these variables. It is also noted, that the exposure environment tends to become less important with increasing age of deposits. In applying Lane and Koelzer method, unit weight of sediment deposited in a given year, at age T years is given by

$$W_{ave} = p_s W_{ts} + p_m W_{tm} + p_c W_{tc} \hspace{2cm} (4.12)$$

where, p = fraction of given size fraction in the deposit and subscript s, m and c stand for sand, silt and clay, respectively. It is recognized that W_{ave} represents spatially averaged value and individual measurements may show considerable deviations. For example,

46

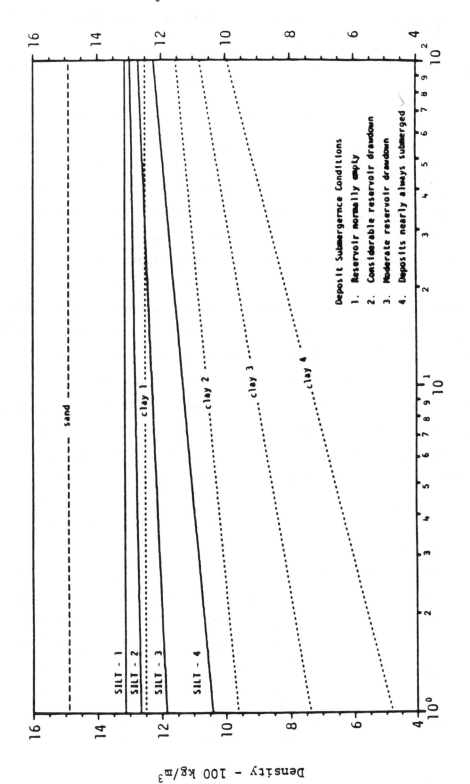

FIG. 4-3 SEDIMENT DEPOSIT IN RESERVOIRS: VARIATION OF DENSITY WITH AGE AND
SUBMERGENCE

Lara and Pemberton (1965) in their analysis of 1316 samples found standard errors of 0.17-0.22 ton/m^3 from their best-fit values.

Delta Formation

The sand and coarser fractions of sediment load entering a reservoir are the first to deposit. The deposits start at the commencement of the backwater curve and the shape of deposit is like a delta. See Fig. 4-4. This part of reservoir deposit is the one most amenable to treatment by channel flow sediment transport theories. Mathematical modeling of delta formation as a part of simulation of reservoir sedimentation is discussed in Chapter V.

As sediment deposition continues, the delta grows in both the upstream and downstream directions by a feedback mechanism. Upstream limit of backwater curve is extended by the initial deposits and so is point of commencement of delta. On the downstream side, longitudinal growth of delta requires sediment transport on top of delta itself. For this reason, after the delta has intruded partly into the reservoir, it will undergo a period of (vertically) upward growth before commencing its downstream migration.

Within the reservoir, the cross-sectional width increases in the downstream direction and except in steep walled, narrow gorges, the width becomes too large for the river current. In such cases, the flow tends to concentrate on a width slightly larger than that of the incoming channel, and the delta growth is temporarily confined to this width. Based on the sedimentation experience at some U.S. reservoirs, Harrison (1983) has described the sequence of delta growth as it fills the reservoir width. As the delta is growing at one location, there will be low-level areas on its side with relatively quiescent water where silts and clays may be deposited. At a certain stage of growth, the current will abandon the earlier delta and move into an adjacent low-level area. It will

48

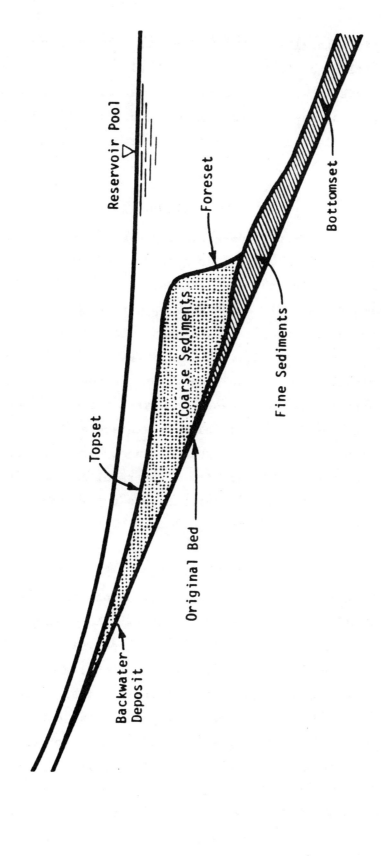

FIG. 4-4 PROFILE OF TYPICAL RESERVOIR DELTA AND NOMENCLATURE FOR DEPOSITS

then fill up this channel and move to another deeper channel. The delta, thus, fills up the valley by lateral avulsions. Harrison (1983) also observes that the sinuosity of channel decreases within the aggrading part of the reservoir so that, ultimately, the channel will follow the valley alignment and not that of the original river channel.

Due to their larger settling velocities, the coarser size fractions of the sediment load--gravels and sands, are the main constituents of delta. However, as stated above, some silts and clays are deposited in the deep channels adjacent to the main current and further, clay flocs may develop within the reservoirs to deposit on the delta itself. The above description of delta formation shows that, primarily, it is a three-dimensional process, which may be simplified to a two-dimensional (along the reservoir and laterally across the width) case. However, the set of governing equations commonly used to model delta growth are a one-dimensional approximation, (See Chapter V), which cannot predict the three-dimensional features of delta deposits. The results computed from a one-dimensional model should be interpreted as the average condition across the reservoir width.

Dead storage in a reservoir is defined as the storage volume between the stream bed and the lowest elevation from which water can be withdrawn by gravity. Conventionally, the dead storage is allocated to the accumulation of sediment deposition within the economic life of the storage. The top of delta develops a slope which is about one-half to two-third of the original slope of the river bed and it is definitely not horizontal. The concept of a dead storage below a horizontal plane, entirely devoted to sediment deposition thus becomes invalid. In fact, a part of the usable capacity will be lost even before the dead storage has been completely filled up. For example, the 1980 survey of Tarbela Reservoir showed that after 6 years of operation, 44 percent of deposit lay in

50

the usable storage zone even though 78 percent of dead storage was still available. Similarly, in the reservoir at High Aswan Dam, approximate analysis of sediment surveys by the writer shows that whereas the total sediment deposit upto 1986 amounts to just under 2 km^3 against a dead storage volume of 31.6 km^3, the net loss of live storage capacity is already more than 1 km^3. At this dam, the total storage capacity is 162 km^3 and, consequently, the recorded loss may not be critical, but it does show the fallacy of computing economic life of a storage on the basis of a uniform rate of depletion of dead storage equal to the volume of annual deposits. This factor should be considered in estimating future usable capacities.

Fine Material Deposit

Discrete particles of silt and clay have rather small settling velocities, Fig. 4-1. Even in the absence of turbulence, these particles can travel considerable distances into a storage reservoir before settling down. As an example, consider a trapezoidal reservoir with a bed width of 100 m, valley side slope of 2H:1V and a bed slope of 0.0002. If 2 micron clay particles enter this reservoir with a flow of 500 m^3/sec, they would travel about 60 km before completely settling down. Under normal circumstances, fine material deposits are, therefore, spread all over the reservoir. They do, however, show size gradation with distance from inlet same as the bed material particles. Two physical aspects of fine material deposits require special mention: the formation of density currents and erosion resistance of clay deposits.

Density Currents

Density currents constitute a special class of flow, where two fluids with similar state and slightly different densities move with respect to each other (Harleman, 1961.) The heavier fluid moving under a lighter fluid is effectively subjected to a reduced gravitational field

$$g' = g (\rho_2 - \rho_1)/\rho_2 \qquad\qquad (4.13)$$

where, ρ_1, ρ_2 = density of the lighter and heavier fluid, respectively.

Storage reservoirs frequently develop density stratifications due to temperature, salinity and turbidity differences between different layers. River flow entering a reservoir may, therefore, develop into an overflow, interflow or underflow depending on its density relative to that of various layers. From sedimentation point of view, the most important of reservoir density currents is the underflow developing due to the relatively higher density of turbid river flow. This, turbidity current, is discussed in the following.

The distinguishing features of turbidity current are: a plunge point, where the river flow dives under the reservoir; a head that forms in the front to provide the potential energy necessary to overcome the inertia of reservoir water ahead of the current and the main density current. The plunge point, Figure 4-5, is the point of separation between the forward moving current and the induced reverse flow in the reservoir. This point is physically marked by collection of floating debris on the reservoir surface. The flow after the plunge point may or may not be uniform and depending on the bed slope, it may develop into a supercritical flow. A certain amount of mixing between the current and reservoir water takes place at the interface. This is not critical, at least in the subcritical flows and turbidity currents are known to maintain their identity over long distances. For example, during the year before the closure of diversion tunnels, density currents travelled through 120 miles length of Lake Mead to deliver about 8.5 million tons of reservoir over a month and a half of turbidity flows (Bell, 1942).

Studies of velocity distribution in the density current head show that there is an upward movement of sediment within the head itself. In the body of the current, however, coarse silt, sand and gravel particles settle down, so that the sediment load transported by a reservoir turbidity current primarily consists of fine silt and clay particles. In Lake Mead 90 % of sediment transported by density currents was smaller than 20 microns and 76 % finer than 5 microns with a current velocity of about 21 cm/sec (Bell, 1942). Similarly, in his laboratory studies, Jia-Hua (1960) found that at current velocities of 4-8 cm/sec, 90 % of sediment lay below 10 microns and 50 % below 3 microns. He also quotes experience on Kuanting Reservoir where, with a current velocity of about 20 cm/sec, 90 % of sediment transported by the density current remained below 130 microns and 50 % below 3 microns. It appears that flocculation of clay particles does not induce settlement of clay out of the density currents.

Realizing the capacity of density currents to convey large concentrations of fine sediments from inlet to the dam, Bell (1942a) made an impassioned plea for selective withdrawal from reservoirs to mitigate siltation. In such a system, the dam would be provided with outlets at different levels from which the turbidity current can be evacuated.

A number of theoretical studies on the dynamics of density currents have been made in the past, e.g., Keulegan, (1944) and (1949); Schijf and Schonfeld (1953); Jia-Hua (1960); Benjamin (1968); Savage and Brimberg (1975); Kao (1977). Most laboratory studies on density currents have been made with salt solutions. Studies using solid particles have been reported by Bell (1942a); Kuenen and Migliorini (1950); Jia-Hua (1960) and, Middleton (1966) among others. Prototype measurements of density currents are even fewer, especially, in large reservoirs. Both Bell (1942) and Howard (1953) have reported data on Lake Mead; Geza and Bogich (1953) have reported measurements on a small water supply and a medium sized hydro-power reservoir; and Jia-Hua (1960) has quoted data from measurements on Kuanting Reservoir. When the density current arrives at the dam, it will rise and be reflected. Effective aspiration of density current requires proper size and location of outlets. Theoretical and experimental studies on the aspiration of density currents have been reported by Yih (1965) and Jia-Hua (1960).

The existence of a plunge point is a necessary condition for the formation of a density current. In general, the condition for the development of a plunge point is

$$F_o = V_o / \sqrt{g' H_o} \qquad (4.14)$$

where, V_o = velocity and H_o = depth of flow at the plunge point. Theoretical value of F_o based on frictionless flow is 0.5. Savage and Brimberg (1975) estimate F_o to lie between 0.3 and 0.8. Jia-Hua (1960) has measured value of 0.78 in laboratory experiments. The ratio of depths at the plunge point to that in the density current according to Jia-Hua's data can be roughly estimated by

$$H_o / H_2 = 0.64 \, F^{0.76} . \qquad (4.15)$$

Under uniform flow conditions, the velocity of density current can be estimated from Darcy-Weisbach friction equation

$$V/U_* = \sqrt{8/f} \qquad (4.16)$$

where, U_*, the shear velocity = $\sqrt{g' H_2 S}$; f = friction factor and S = bed slope. Measured value of f for the lower boundary of the flow lie between 0.020 and 0.025 and it should be increased by about 0.005 to account for the additional shear force at the interface.

Erosion of Fine Material

In contrast with the bed material, the erosion or, for that matter, the deposition of fine material depends much more on the interparticle physico-chemical forces than on the particle size itself. For this reason, the concept of critical shear stress as a relation between mechanical forces tending to entrain the particle in the bed and the granular friction tending to resist the motion, (Chapter IV, Entrainment), is no longer valid.

The forces required to keep the fine particles in suspension are almost negligible. Given appropriate mineral structure of clay and water, clay particle colliding with each other will form flocs which are a loose lattice of clay particles with a variable degree of bonding forces. Flocs have larger settling velocity than individual particles and as they settle to the lower flow boundary, those with weaker strength are sheared again. Once the flocs deposit in the bed, they form floc aggregates and aggregate networks, which are still characterized by low density and a small shear strength. With increasing overburden, the interparticle distance is reduced and the bonding force is considerably increased.

The present (1986) understanding of deposition and erosion of fine material has largely come from the extensive work done by Partheniades (1972) in this field. Due to large variation of relevant conditions in storage reservoirs, it is not possible at this time to specify critical entrainment conditions for silt and clays. In the mathematical modeling of reservoirs with significant fine material load, two critical values are commonly defined. One, for the threshold of deposition and the other, for threshold of erosion. Typical value for the former are 0.5-1.0 N/m^2 and those for erosion are 5-10 N/m^2. The following qualitative principles are useful in understanding the deposition and erosion behavior of clays.

If an initial concentration of clay particles is introduced in a flow, it will soon develop an equilibrium concentration which is nearly uniform along the depth and which is a constant fraction of the initial value. This constant is a function of the boundary shear stress and the clay mineralogy and as shown by Partheniades' experiments, it is sensitive to small changes in temperature and chemical composition of water. Once the material has been deposited, the shear stress required to reentrain the particles is much larger than that required to prevent its deposition. Further, the critical shear stress for erosion increases with the age and compaction of deposit. The gross soil mechanics parameters for describing the strength of soils, such as shear strength, cohesion, dry density and Atterberg limits do not correlate with the initiation or rate of erosion, except in a limiting sense.

The erosion resistance of aged clay deposits in reservoirs is well known. In river mechanics, the role played by old clay plugs has been emphasized by Winkley (1977) and Mahmood (1963) has described the problems created by clay layers in the development of man-made cutoffs. Harrison (1983) cites his observation on South Canadian River, where an old clay layer was exposed after about 3 m cut through sandy stratum and it would not erode even though the flow was competent to move cobbles.

CHAPTER V

PREDICTIVE METHODS FOR RESERVOIR SEDIMENTATION

The engineering interest in reservoir sedimentation primarily concerns three physical aspects: total volume of trapped sediment; spatial distribution of deposit volume and, sediment load carried by flow releases including its particle size distribution. The volume of deposit represents loss of storage capacity which reduces the efficacy of a reservoir to regulate flow. The distribution of deposit determines the relative impact of trapped sediments on the usable storage as well as the prospect of flushing it. The sediment load carried by flow releases is the potential source of abrasion damage to power turbines and outlet works.

At the design stage, sediment load data for the stream are expressed as seasonal rating functions of flow discharge. The load may be measured in units of mass per unit time or as concentration in the flow , e.g., ppm. The sediment inflow hydrograph to the reservoir is then computed from the rating functions and flow hydrograph. Part of the sediment inflow, that will be trapped in the reservoir is calculated and with an estimated mass density for the deposit, it is converted to the volume of deposit. The estimation of density is an important step in this process because any uncertainty in its value directly translates into a corresponding uncertainty in the volume of sediment deposit.

Methods used to predict various aspects of reservoir sedimentation can be broadly divided into two classes: empirical methods that are founded on fairly correct understanding of the physical processes but are based on the inductive analysis of data and, mathematical models that are based on an analytical treatment of hydraulic and sedimentary processes in the reservoir. Neither of them is presently equipped to completely handle all of the three areas of engineering interest and in practice a combination of the two is used. Existing mathematical models will use the empirical methods for estimation of density of deposits because a theoretical model for this does not exist. Similarly, the present day empirical methods cannot predict the concentration and particle size distribution of sediment carried by flow releases from a reservoir. This information, if required, must be obtained from an appropriate mathematical model.

Most mathematical models are based on coupled or sequential application of one-dimensional equations of motion for the water phase and equation of mass conservation for the sediment. A few exploratory attempts have been made to use two-dimensional models based on sediment diffusion equation. Currently available methods for predicting various aspects of reservoir sedimentation, both empirical and mathematical models, are described in this chapter to elucidate their scope and limitations.

Trap Efficiency of Reservoirs

Trap efficiency of reservoirs is defined as the proportion of incoming sediment load that is retained in the reservoir. Empirical methods to predict trap efficiency of reservoirs are represented by the graphical techniques developed by Churchill (1947), Brune (1953) and Heinemann (1981). Of these, the Brune's curve, Figure 5-1, is most popular in practice mainly because it uses a rather simple and readily available predictor. The independent parameter in this method is the volume ratio of reservoir storage to annual water inflow and the dependent variable is trap efficiency. Factors such as reservoir shape and frequency of drawdown are not considered. Churchill's curves are based on a more appropriate parameter, called sedimentation index. This is defined as the average retention time divided by the mean velocity of flow in the reservoir. Heinemann

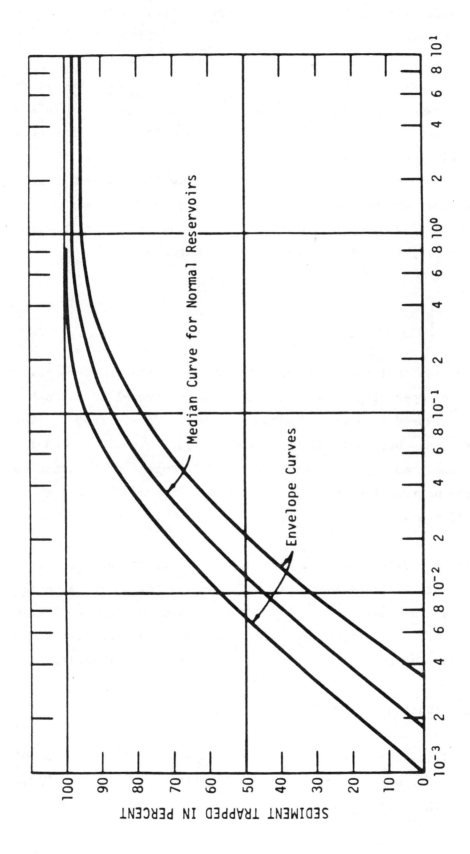

CAPACITY - INFLOW RATIO

FIG. 5-1 BRUNE'S CURVE FOR RESERVOIR TRAP EFFICIENCY

curve is a revision of Brune curve for reservoirs with catchment areas less than 40 km^2.

Brune's curve is based on data obtained from 44 reservoirs covering drainage areas of 4 - 480,000 km^2. The capacity: inflow ratio in his data varies from 0.0016 to 4.65 and the trap efficiency from 0 to 100 percent. In the analysis of his data, Brune made a distinction between reservoirs that are normally ponded, i.e., operated without any effort to sluice sediment; those where sluicing has been used as an operational policy and, the desilting basins. His median curve, (Fig. 5-1), can be approximated by

$$T = 100. \left[1 - \frac{1}{222.92 \log (V(H_m)/I)} \right] \qquad (5.1)$$

where, T = trap efficiency in percent; $V(H_m)$ = reservoir capacity upto H_m = mean operating level, and I = average annual flow. Both V and I are expressed in similar units of volume. This method, or for that matter the Churchill and Heinemann curves, cannot be used for durations less than a year. According to U.S. Bureau of Reclamation (1977), the period of computation for Brune's method should not be less than 10 years.

Heinemann's data show that Brune's curve overestimates the trap efficiency of small reservoirs to some extent. In general, reservoirs with storage capacity larger than about 0.1 km^3 will trap nearly 100 percent of incoming load. In practical applications, Brune's median curve should be treated as a good approximation.

Spatial Distribution of Deposits

An empirical method to predict the spatial distribution of deposits is given by U.S. Bureau of Reclamation (1977). The "Area Reduction Method" is based on the premise that sediment load in a narrow reservoir will travel farther, because the average velocity of flow will be higher than in a wide reservoir. Moreover, a steep, narrow reservoir has a better chance of developing density currents than one that is wide and flat. This qualitative reasoning is used to develop four classes of reservoirs, Table 5-1, depending on their morphology. The latter is measured by a single parameter m given by

$$V(h) = a \ h^m \tag{5.2}$$

where, h = height measured above the river bed at the dam axis.

Table 5-1

RESERVOIR CLASSIFICATION AND DISTRIBUTION PARAMETERS
(U.S.B.R. Area Reduction Method)

Type	Class	m in Eq. (5.2)	p	q	B(1+p,1+q)
I	Lake	3.5 - 4.5	1.85	0.36	5.047
II	Floodplain-foothill	2.5 - 3.5	0.57	0.41	2.487
III	Hill	1.5 - 2.5	-1.15	2.32	16.967
IV	Gorge	1.0 - 1.5	-0.25	1.34	1.486

The basic assumption used in this method is that the relative area of deposits is distributed as a Beta function of the relative depth as

$$A_* = h_*^p \ \frac{(1 - h_*)^q}{B(1 + p, 1 + q)} \tag{5.3}$$

where,

$$A_* (h_*) = \frac{A(h)}{A_{ref}} , \tag{5.4}$$

$$h_* = \frac{h}{H_c} , \tag{5.5}$$

$B(.,.)$ = Beta function, parameters p and q are functions of reservoir class, See Table 5-1, $A(h)$ = surface area of deposit at elevation h, A_{ref} = parametric area of deposit and, H_c = value of h for the active conservation pool level. The vertical distribution of volume of deposit, V_d is a function of h, as

$$V_d(h) = \int_o^h A(y) \, dy \quad ; \quad h \leq H_c \tag{5.6}$$

and, the total volume of deposits upto the active conservation level is $V_d(H_c)$. The value of parameter A_{ref} can be computed from the fact that for the level of deposit at the dam axis, the surface area of deposit is equal to the surface area of the reservoir itself. This condition is expressed as

$$\frac{V_d(H_c) - V_d(h_o)}{H_c \, A(h_o)} = \frac{1}{A_*(h_{*o})} \left[1 - \frac{V_d(h_o)}{V_d(H_c)} \right] \tag{5.7}$$

where, h_o = height of deposit at the dam axis and $h_{*o} = h_o/H_c$. Both the left and right hand sides of Eq. (5.7) represent the average height of deposits above h_o, taken as the prismatic volume above $A(h_o)$ and, expressed as a fraction of H_c. The left hand side is a function of reservoir morphology and h_o and, the right hand side is a function of parameters, p and q and h_{*o}. Eq. (5.7) is solved by trial and error for h_{*o}. The corresponding value of A_{ref} is obtained from Eq. (5.3) and of A_{*o} from Eq. (5.4). Values of A_* are then

62

calculated for other values of h_* and the volume of deposits from bed upward is computed by numerical integration. A step by step procedure for the above method based on graphs of Beta functions is given in U.S. Bureau of Reclamation (1977).

Reservoir pool level is a fluctuating quantity. The distribution given by the area reduction method is based on the volume accumulated upto the top of active conservation pool. A part of deposit, related to the sediment inflow during floods, will be located above the active conservation level, H_c. This has to be separately estimated and the above method applied to the balance distributed between $0 \leq h \leq H_c$. The proportion of total deposit above H_c will be larger for reservoirs that have a greater component of storage capacity allocated to flood control and this may sometime reduce the utility of area reduction method inasmuch as it does not treat the volume of deposit above H_c.

The area-reduction method has been based on data obtained from 30 reservoirs. It does not account for temporary or prolonged reservoir drawdown brought about as an operational necessity or as a deliberate sediment sluicing operation. Also, it does not consider the sediment size distribution as a factor in the problem. In practice, these conditions can be accounted for by shifting the computed reservoir class in Table 5-1 upward or downward. For example, if the fine material constitutes a large component of the sediment load, or if the reservoir experiences considerable drawdown, its class should be shifted downward.

Frequently, a reservoir will not have a unique value of m for its entire depth. In such cases, the reservoir class in Table 5-1 is selected on the basis of m value in the segment where most of the deposit will occur. A problem in selecting the reservoir class is also experienced in compound reservoirs. The only recourse in that case is to use some judgment in selecting the reservoir class and to apportion the volume of deposit to each segment of the reservoir (Dorough, 1986).

This method is to be applied to the distribution of deposits accumulated over long periods, such as a few decades and not for the year-to-year accumulation. Application of the method to reservoirs that significantly differ in design, operation and sediment characteristics from those used in its derivation may yield substantially inaccurate results.

Mathematical Models

Mathematical analysis of sedimentation transients is based on the premise that the dynamic action of flow acting through sediment transport is the driving force and sediment deposit (or scour) takes place due to the spatial variations in the transport rate. As the sediment transients move at a much small rate compared to the celerity of water waves, the discharge can be considered to be steady during the time interval used to compute scour/deposition [e.g., Mahmood, (1975), Chen, et al (1975)]. Given this simplification, the govern-ing equations for the sediment transient are

Equations of Motion:

$$\frac{\partial}{\partial t}\left(\frac{Q}{gA}\right) + \frac{\partial}{\partial x}\left(\frac{Q^2}{2gA^2} + y\right) + S_f = 0 \tag{5.8}$$

Equation of Continuity of the Bed Material:

$$\frac{\partial G_b}{\partial x} + \frac{\partial G_s}{\partial x} + \frac{\partial}{\partial t}(C_s A) + p_* \frac{\partial}{\partial t}(B_d z) = 0 \tag{5.9}$$

where, Q = discharge; g = gravitational acceleration; A = area of cross section; y = water surface elevation; S_f = energy gradient;

64

G_b = bed load; G_s = suspended load; C_s = average spatial sediment concentration in the cross-section; p_* = density of sediment in the bed; B_d = the deformable bed width; z = bed elevation; x = distance along the channel bed measured in the downstream direction and, t = time.

Eqs. (5.8) and (5.9) form a set of hyperbolic equations. They require two supplementary equations. One relating S_f and the other relating sediment transport quantities: G_b, G_s and C_s, to the flow and sediment size values. For uniqueness, they also require the initial conditions and boundary conditions to be specified. In reservoir sedimentation, the accuracy of initial conditions is not very critical because they are overtaken by the deposition process. At the downstream end, hydrograph of reservoir pool elevation provides appropriate boundary condition and at the upstream end, the discharge and sediment inflow hydrographs provide the necessary boundary conditions. The model results are very sensitive to the sediment inflow boundary condition and to the accuracy of supplementary equations used to compute sediment transport quantities.

The above equations constitute a one-dimensional representation of sediment transients. They can be solved by one of the finite difference schemes. In implicit formulations (e.g., Mahmood and Ponce, 1976), that solve the two equations simultaneously over the total space domain, the numerical stability problems are much smaller but, the development of computer program is more expensive. In a simple, sequential-explicit formulation, the dynamic Eq. (5.9) is first reduced to steady nonuniform flow by dropping out the unsteady term. It is solved by backwater computation methods and is followed by the calculation of bed level changes through Eq. (5.10). The advantage is a rather simple solution algorithm but numerical stability considerations will require small time steps. Total computational time, however, may or may not be larger than the implicit method. Other advantages of this method are that any sediment transport function, irrespective of its complexity can be used in the computer analysis and channel networks can be easily handled.

Another consideration in mathematical modeling of reservoir sedimentation is that because of strong hydraulic sorting of sediment sizes in reservoirs, bookkeeping of sediment deposit is to be maintained by various grain size fractions at different elevations in the deposit. This is necessary to realistically model the reentrainment of deposits under lower pool elevations and is especially critical if the size distribution of sediment is such that an armor layer may develop during sediment reentrainment phase. Such a bookkeeping is much easier done with the sequential-explicit algorithms. The most popular and commonly available program package, based on this algorithm, is U.S Army Corps of Engineers' HEC-6 program (1977). HEC-6 provides for bookkeeping of deposits by various particle size classes and any sediment transport function appropriate to the conditions at a site can be built into it. This model has been adapted to the special conditions at proposed Kalabagh Dam for investigations relating to Project Planning Report, executed under the World Bank supervision (Pakistan WAPDA, 1984).

A major difficulty in the application of available reservoir sedimentation models arises from the fact that none of the available bed material load functions has been tested on deep reservoirs flows or for the degree of nonuniformity of flow experienced in large reservoirs. Toffaleti's method (1969), among all of the available functions, is based on the largest range of flow depths but even that falls short of the depth found in large reservoirs. The bed material load functions are, also, deficient in their treatment of fine material load (Chapter IV). In most sandbed rivers, this is a serious handicap because 50 percent or more of the total load in these streams lies in clay-silt size range. In general, the bed

66

transient models will adequately simulate the sedimentation processes over the delta but downstream of that their reliability is questionable. These difficulties have given rise to another type of models that treat the reservoirs as desilting basins.

Hurst and Chao (1975) abandoned the one-dimensional transient model in their planning studies for Tarbela Dam. Instead, they adopted Camp's (1944) trap efficiency curves for desilting basins. Such a model will most likely succeed in the early life of reservoirs that do not experience significant drawdown. When the delta has formed in the reservoir and at least part of the reservoir flow is of riverine type, the method will fail because desilting basin models, such as Camp's, are based on the assumption that the lower boundary of the basin is an absorbing boundary with no reentrainment. The operational experience at Tarbela shows that Hurst and Chao's analysis grossly under-estimated the streamwise progression of delta. The actual delta crest after 9 years operation was located about 12 miles upstream of the dam instead of 30 miles predicted by their model. This is directly attributable to the afore mentioned reason.

A sediment diffusion model has been used by Merrill (1980) to simulate the sedimentation in three reservoirs in Nebraska and Illinois in which 90 percent of sediment load consists of clay-silt sizes. This model is based on two dimensional diffusion equation solved by an explicit numerical scheme. The reservoir is divided into cells of similar area in plan and incoming sediment load is routed through these cells from the inlet to the outlet. The diffusion constant is a key parameter of the problem and it was empirically computed from the available reservoir sedimentation data. The conceptual approach of Merrill's study is appropriate and it shows that diffusion type models can be applied to reservoir sedimentation where the primary sediment load is in clay-silt range and reentrainment of deposits is not present. At present (1986),

67

realistic values of sediment diffusion coefficient in reservoir flows are not available and the erosion functions for silt and clays, that are important in fine material dominant streams are not sufficiently known.

Evaluation

Reservoir sedimentation is a complex phenomenon in the sense that definitive knowledge on many of its physical processes is not available. Examples of processes that strongly influence the form and location of deposits but which cannot be predicted with sufficient certainty are: three dimensional nature of flow; chemical regimes and stratification in the reservoir; three dimensional features of density currents; flocculation of clays; fall properties of flocs and, threshold conditions as well as rate of reentrainment of fine material deposits.

Two primary inputs to the reservoir, water discharge and sediment load, naturally vary from year to year and in certain cases, catastrophic events in a catchment may impose unprecedented loading, far different from the average. The use of a reservoir is bound to undergo some change during its lifetime and more importantly, economic factors may evolve in the future with a consequent shift in the project objectives. Under these circumstances, predictive methods in reservoir design analysis can only be expected to provide a statistically averaged answer based on the present perception of the future. In the actual future, csubstantial deviations from the present predictions may occur because, there is no control on the magnitude and sequence of future inputs and, future operation policies may differ from those assumed at the design stage.

With the increasing age of world reservoirs, their problem of siltation is currently in the fore front. There is a greater emphasis on prolonging the life of reservoirs both in the design of new projects and in the operation of existing structures. Predictive methods are needed to evaluate the performance of measures such as sediment sluicing and flushing used to alleviate the rate of reservoir sedimentation. Also, there are new areas of concern such as the particle size distribution of sediment carried by flow releases that were not quantitatively treated in the past. The evaluation of empirical and mathematical modeling techniques has to be viewed in this context.

The essential difference between the empirical and mathematical modeling techniques for reservoir sedimentation lies in their scope. The empirical techniques are simple and mostly graphic. They are expected to yield an approximate answer. They do not require advanced technical skills or computers in their application. Hence, they are relatively inexpensive to use. Empirical models cannot be used to predict the time-dependent behavior of reservoirs within a yearly cycle or even, over a few years. Also, they are not suitable for special operational conditions applicable to mitigative measures discussed in Chapter VI.

The mathematical models, on the other hand, are broader in scope. They require specialist technical inputs and computational skills and more importantly, they require considerably greater data inputs. They are, consequently, two to three orders of magnitude more expensive than the empirical methods. In contrast with their empirical counterparts, properly developed and calibrated mathematical models can be used to analyze time-dependent behavior of reservoirs, including special conditions imposed by sediment sluicing and flushing operations (See, Chapter VI). At the current (1986) state of-the-art, mathematical models are based on hydraulic resistance and sediment transport functions that have been derived from open channel flow. Their applicability to the deep flow in storage reservoirs has not been investigated so far. Bed material type transport functions derived from channel flows are not expected to apply to the fine material load which is the dominant fraction and which plays an important role in reservoirs. The lack of knowledge on the reentrainment of clays after they have initially deposited in reservoirs and the sensitivity of density current formation to thermal and chemical regimes of impounded waters, also, makes the results of present day mathematical models approximate to an extent.

Many small projects, cannot bear the cost of detailed investigations by mathematical models and will have to rely on the empirical models. On most of the large projects, engineering investigations, involving simultaneous applications of different mathematical models for various components of the problem and some original investigations will be found to be economically justifiable. There is a need to improve the accuracy of both the empirical methods and mathematical models. This is discussed in Chapter VII.

CHAPTER VI

MITIGATION OF RESERVOIR SILTATION

Loss of reservoir storage to siltation is the primary concern in this monograph. Reservoirs have other sediment related impacts on the river channel upstream and downstream, such as retrogression of river bed level on the downstream side and the aggradation and flooding on the upstream side. Some of these adverse effects are also mitigated if the accumulation of sediment within the reservoir is reduced. For example, if the incoming load is flushed through, the channel deterioration is ameliorated to a large extent. In this chapter, the mitigation of loss of storage to sediment accumulation remains to be the main concern. Benefits accruing to other areas will, however, be identified where applicable.

The methods for controlling reservoir sedimentation can be divided into three categories. The first category consists of methods that reduce sediment inflow into the reservoirs. These are: control of sediment generation through watershed management; retention of sediment in debris basins before the river enters the reservoir and, bypassing sediment. The second category consist of methods that use hydraulics of flow to reduce the accumulation of load that has entered the reservoir. Sediment flushing operations, sediment sluicing through specially designed reservoir operation policies and release of density currents belong to this category. The third category consists of hydraulic dredging of existing sediment deposits. All of these methods have been tried to some extent and, generally, none of them will provide a complete mitigation. These methods, their scope and limitations are discussed in the following.

Watershed Management

Intuitively, the first method of reducing reservoir siltation would be to reduce sediment yield from the basin upstream of the reservoir by watershed management. Such a scheme would involve afforestation, land use change and construction of micro structures to control gulley erosion and to trap sediment. The forests are an indispensable component of world's ecological system. As such, watershed management as a means to provide sediment control in reservoirs always finds strong moral support. Facts, on the other hand do not support its efficacy, as far as reservoirs are concerned.

The world average for sediment load concentration is less than 500 ppm, (See Chapter III, page 26). This is almost an ideal situation for reservoirs. With this concentration, a storage built with a gross volume equal to mean annual flow will lose less than 0.04 percent of volume to siltation each year, compared to about 1 percent of the estimated average rate of siltation of world dams. Consideration of sediment load in world rivers in Chapter III has shown that high concentrations of sediment are largely associated with climatic, tectonic and geological factors. The effectiveness of human actions in controlling these processes is doubtful. There is the additional factor of watershed acting as a strong low pass filter which dampens the space and time variations of sediment generation within the basin. Coon Creek data (Chapter III--Human Impact on Sediment Yield) appear to support the conclusion one would draw from the physical processes operative in drainage basins, that over periods of engineering or economic interest, the sediment yields are largely unaffected by watershed management. The sediment sources within the basin, including its hillslopes, valley floors and river channels will amply make up for whatever reduction of erosion can be effected by watershed control. A case in point is Mangla watershed in Pakistan, where an extensive watershed management project was initiated before the construction of dam.

Mangla Dam is a multipurpose, 112 m high earth-rockfill dam on Jhelum River in Pakistan with a crest level of 376.1 m. The design maximum reservoir elevation is 374.3 m, the top of conservation pool is at elevation 366.4 m and that of the dead capacity at 317.0 m. The total storage capacity of the reservoir to elevation 374.3 is 9.47 km^3; usable capacity from elevation 317.0 to 366.4 is 6.58 km^3 and the dead capacity is 0.67 km^3. The catchment area of Mangla is 33,333 km^2. A schematic of Mangla catchment, including gaging stations, is shown in Fig. 6-1. Also shown in this figure are sub-catchment areas, their mean annual flow and measured suspended load concentration for WAPDA's 1970-75 data (Rehman, A., undated). Relevant data for sub-catchments are tabulated in Table 6-1. It is seen that of the gaged streams, Kanshi River brings in the highest concentration of sediment followed by Kunhar and Punch, both of which have roughly equal concentrations. The main sediment contribution of 73.4 percent comes from area below Kohala which contributes only 11.7 percent of flow volume.

Two reservoir sedimentation surveys were carried out in Mangla reservoir during 1970 and 1973. They measured average annual deposit of 0.037 km^3. According to its design operation, the reservoir is filled up in late August when most of the heavy sediment concentration has passed. Field inspections have shown no backwater deposits at the reservoir inlets. Power inlets are located about 31 m above the original river bed. Sediment concentrations have been periodically measured in the power flow and generally average about 25 ppm. Larger concentrations associated with high river flows have been measured up to 430 ppm (river flow = 11,160 m^3/sec; reservoir level = 365m). They are, probably, associated with weak density currents. The average trap efficiency of the reservoir is estimated to be around 99 percent.

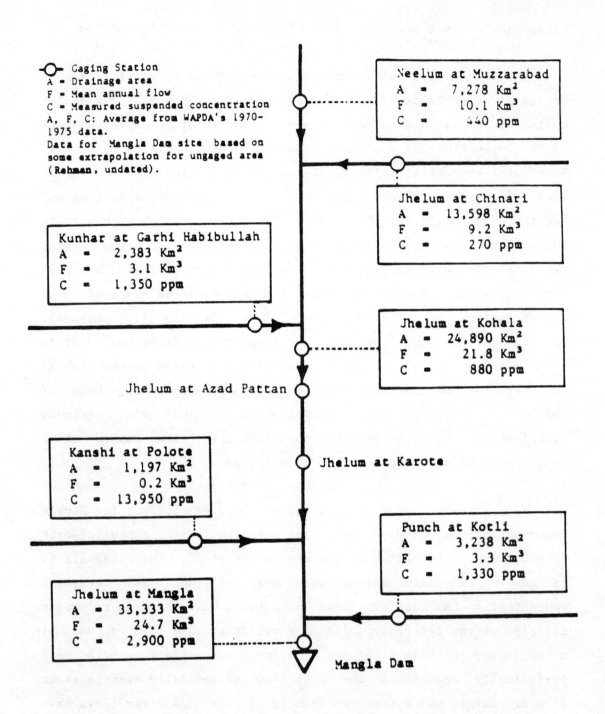

FIG. 6-1 SCHEMATIC CATCHMENT OF RIVER JHELUM AT MANGLE DAM

Table 6-1

MANGLA DAM CATCHMENT:
MEAN ANNUAL WATER AND SEDIMENT
CONTRIBUTIONS (1970 - 1975)

River	Station	Drainage Area (km^2)	Flow			Measured Suspended Sediment Load		
			km^3	cm	%	10 tons	C	%
Neelum	Muzaffabad	7,278	10.1	139	40.9	4.4	440	6.2
Jhelum	Chinari	13,598	9.2	68	37.4	2.5	270	3.5
Kunhar	Garhi Habibullah	2,383	3.1	130	12.6	4.2	1350	5.9
Jhelum	Kohala	24,890	21.8	88	88.3	19.1	880	26.6
Kanshi	Polote	1,197	0.2	17	0.6	2.2	13,950	3.0
Punch	Kotli	3,238	3.3	102	13.5	4.4	1,330	6.2
Jhelum	Mangla	33,333	24.7	74	100.0	71.5	2,900	100.0

Notes:

1. Data adapted from Rehman (undated). In the original, data for Mangla are based on extrapolations for un-gaged area, which may be in error. For example, annual flow volumes at Mangla always less than the partial sum: (Jhelum at Kohala + Kanshi at Polote + Punch at Kotli). Similarly, the estimated sediment load at Mangla is significantly higher than surveyed deposit volumes. Numerical values of flows and sediment load at Mangla should be viewed with caution. Percent values for sub-catchments are judged to be representative.

2. Percentages refer to values at Mangla.

3. All values rounded off.

A brief description of various sub-catchments at Mangla Dam (Pakistan WAPDA, 1961) follows:

River Neelum rises at about 5,200 m elevation and has a gradient of about 1.86 percent in 240 km length. A significant part of its runoff originates in the glaciers and permanent snow fields of Nanga Parbat Massif. Mean annual precipitation in its catchment is about 150 cm.

River Kunhar rises at an elevation of about 4,270 m. Glaciers and small ice fields of Kaghan with mountain peaks around 5,000 m elevation, are an important source of its water supply. In its upper 130 km, the river has a slope of about 1.89 percent. Mean annual precipitation in its catchment is about 150 cm.

River Jhelum at Chinari passes through a number of lakes in Kashmir Valley where it loses most of its sediment load. In the last 130 kms, it has a gradient of about 0.62 percent. Mean annual precipitation in this catchment is around 120 cm.

Kanshi River rises in gravel uplands at an elevation of about 760 m. It has an average gradient of about 0.47 percent. Average annual precipitation in this catchment is around 95 cm.

Punch River rises at an elevation of about 3,050 m. Over a length of about 130 km, it has a gradient of about 1.89 percent.

A watershed management project was prepared for Mangla in 1959. This comprised two sub areas. An area of 7,640 km^2, in the lower catchment, considered to be the most serious sediment contributor, was selected for priority treatment. This area was photographed and mapped for land use and capability. Another area of about 7,800 km^2 covering the northern tributaries of Neelum and Kunhar was considered to be less serious and it was not photographed. Most of the rocks in the study area are inherently erodible--from the unconsolidated loess to the limestones and schists which have suffered continual disturbance by earth movement. The overall geologic erosion is judged to be high due to precipitous hill slopes. The vegetal cover, even at high altitudes, has been disturbed by human activity, to an extent that it is ineffective against erosion. In the priority area, good protective forest covers less than one percent of the area.

The management project comprising a large number of structural and non-structural measures in the priority area, started in 1959-60 with the primary objective of reducing the sediment load at Mangla. It was anticipated that as a result of the project, sediment load at Mangla will reduce by about 30 percent, with most of the reduction effected in the loads contributed by Kanshi and Punch Rivers. The project also aimed at ameliorating local environmental conditions and improving productivity. The 30-year project has been phased into a seven-year demonstration phase (1959 - 1966), followed by a 23-year operation phase. Estimated total cost of project, up to 1988, is Rs 339.3 millions.

In order to evaluate the effect of project on sediment load, discharge and measured suspended sediment data for 4 stations in Mangla catchment are shown in Figs. 6-2 thru 6-5. They have been extracted from published stream gaging data. In each case, no discernible difference in the sediment loads is noted over a period of 4-14 years of treatment. Note that, Figs. 6-4 and 6-5 pertain to measured sediment data in Kanshi and Punch rivers, especially targeted for the management activity, with time lapse of 11 and 14 hears, respectively. Judged from the trend of measured sediment data and Coon Creek experience (Chapter III) the impact of watershed management plan on the sediment load at Mangla Dam is likely to be insignificant. That is, not to say, however, that this project is

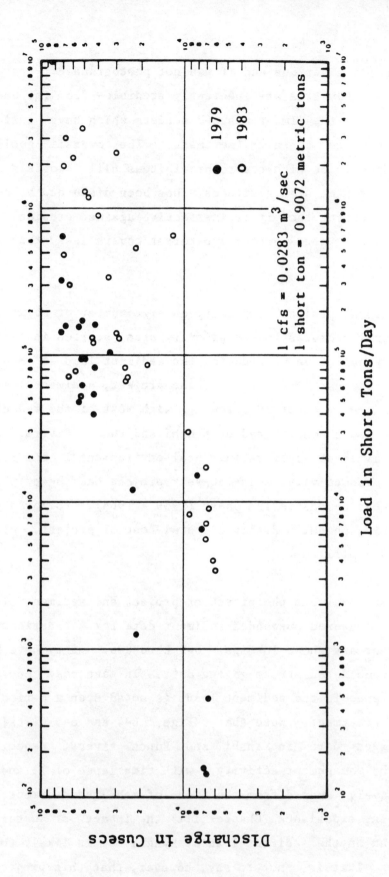

FIG. 6-2 MEASURED SUSPENDED LOAD FOR JHELUM RIVER AT AZAD PATTAN: 1979 AND 1983 DATA

78

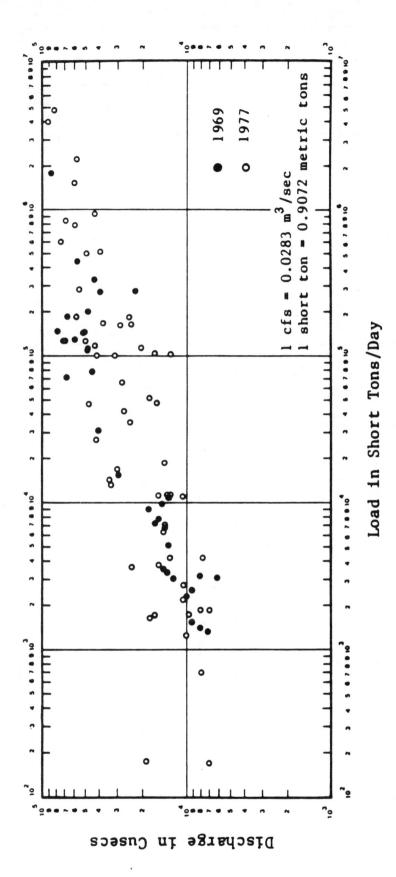

FIG. 6-3   MEASURED SUSPENDED LOAD FOR JHELUM RIVER AT KAROT:
1969 AND 1979 DATA

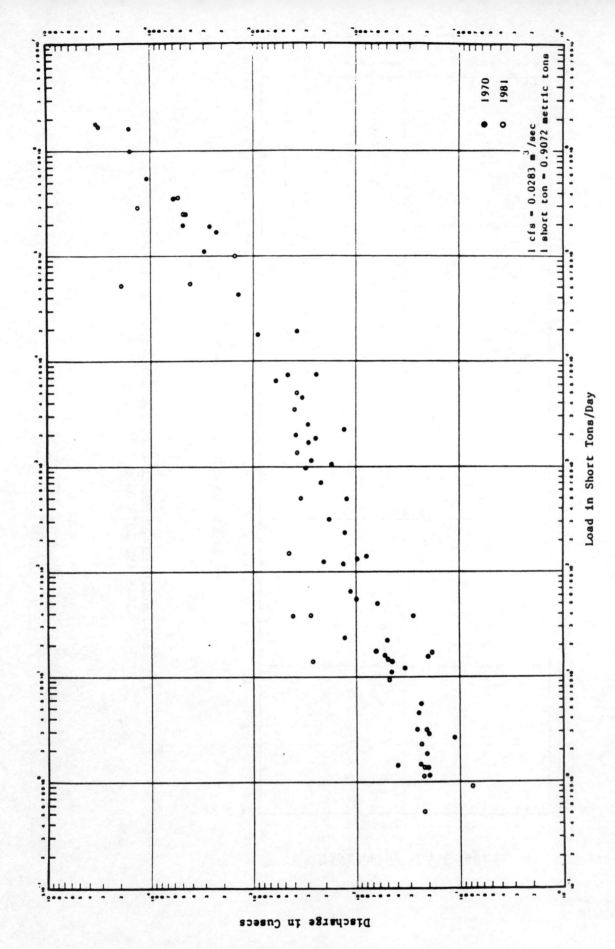

Discharge in Cusecs

Load in Short Tons/Day

1970
1981

1 cfs = 0.0283 m³/sec
1 short ton = 0.9072 metric tons

FIG. 6-4 MEASURED SUSPENDED LOAD FOR KANSHI RIVER NEAR PALOTE: 1970 AND 1981 DATA

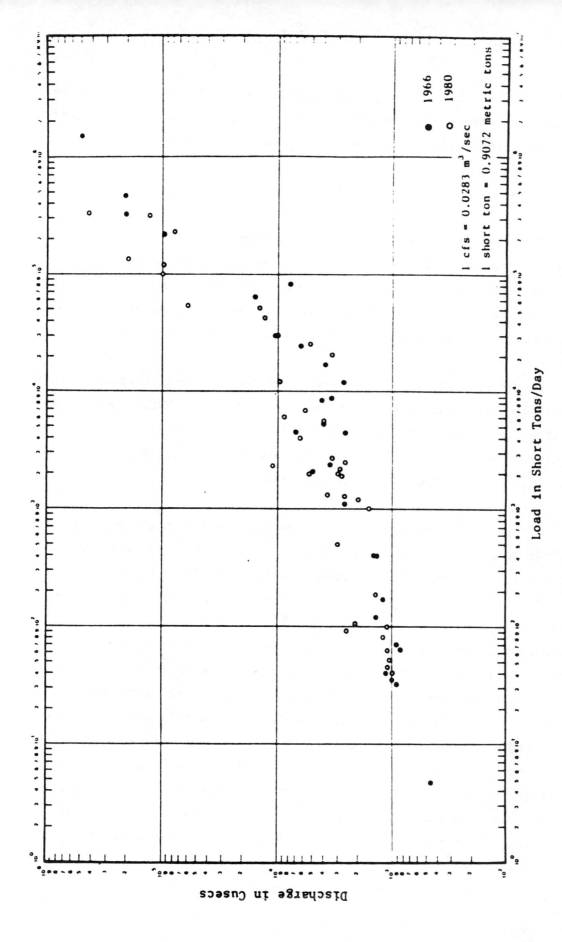

Load in Short Tons/Day

Discharge in Cusecs

1966
1980

● 1966
○ 1980

1 cfs = 0.0283 m³/sec
1 short ton = 0.9072 metric tons

FIG. 6-5 MEASURED SUSPENDED LOAD FOR PUNCH RIVER NEAR KOTLI:
1966 AND 1980 DATA

81

not useful or that it is unproductive. Its beneficial impact on the local environment and productivity must be high; but, in the context of Mangla reservoir sedimentation, its contribution is doubtful.

Debris Dams

The concept of a debris dam is to control the sediment inflow into a reservoir by damming up one or more of its main sediment contributing tributaries. Debris dams are generally much smaller than the main dam. However, for their own safety, they are provided with spillway structures of appropriate discharge capacity.

Experience with the silting up of two sediment reservoirs on mountain streams is given by Armatov et al (1974). These reservoirs silt up faster than the main dam and due to their smaller capacity, sediment deposits in such reservoirs approach the original river bed material more so than in the larger reservoirs.

In general, two factors work against the economic viability of debris dams. One is their short life and the second is the economy of scale. The larger the sediment concentration in a tributary, the smaller will be the life of a debris dam built on it. A significant portion of the cost of a storage is related to the foundation treatment at the dam and the construction of appurtenant structures, such as spillways. The storage at a debris dam is short lived and it is not expected to reduce the design flood at the main dam. In general, a debris dam provides no relief to the main dam except in the sediment storage capacity. The cost of a debris dam is, therefore, to be weighed against the provision of an equivalent storage in the main dam and, the latter is generally much cheaper. Debris dams are sometimes found to be useful in retaining the coarse material, which may induce serious problems due to backwater deposit in the main reservoir.

Sediment Bypassing

Conceptually, it is possible to bypass a portion of the incoming sediment load around the storage. This has been attempted on small irrigation reservoirs (Urlapov, 1977). The flood flows in this case are passed through the main channel, while the irrigation supplies are stored in a reservoir formed on the flood plain.

In large reservoirs, the difficulties of handling large volumes of flow in sediment excluding structures and in locating areas for sediment disposal require a bold design approach, which has not been attempted. The size distribution of sediment load is also a critical factor in the design of bypassing works. In general, it is not possible to remove significant quantities of silts and clay through sediment excluders. Of the sand load, the excluders can optimally remove only about half of the load with one-tenth of the flow. A variant of sediment bypassing is the off-channel storage reservoirs. In these reservoirs, sediment exclusion can be achieved by sediment excluders for coarse material and by shutting off diversion during floods.

Sediment Flushing

Sediment flushing is, herein, used to describe the method of hydraulically clearing existing sediment accumulation in a dam, possibly, through a low-level outlet. In these operations, it is sometimes erroneously assumed that merely releasing the flow will erode the deposits which can be flushed through the outlet structures. To understand the operation of sediment flushing, one refers to the sediment continuity Eq. (5.9), rewritten, after dropping out the spatial concentration term, as:

$$\frac{\partial G}{\partial x} + B_d P_\star \frac{\partial z}{\partial t} = 0 \qquad\qquad (6.1)$$

where, G = total sediment transport and other terms have been defined under Eq.(5.10). Equation (6.1) states that the time rate of lowering of bed level, z, is proportional to the spatial rate of change in G. Thus, at any cross-section

$$\frac{\partial z}{\partial t} = - \frac{1}{B_d P_*} \frac{\partial G}{\partial x} \; .$$ (6.2)

With a given flushing discharge, in a reservoir with level pool, G decreases along the direction of flow, because the area of cross section increases and the velocity decreases. Thus,   and would be greater than 0. That is, with a level pool, the deposits in the upper reaches tends to aggrade. In the lower and deeper parts of reservoir, where G = 0 and $\frac{\partial G}{\partial x}$ = 0, there will be no change in the elevation of deposit. This is the typical process of deposit formation in reservoirs so that with a level pool, flushing will not move the main bulk of deposits any closer to the outlets.

As the low-level outlets are first opened in a reservoir with a level pool, the local concentration of flow entrains the fine material deposits close to the outlet. This gives a false impression to a lay observer of extensive desilting of the reservoir. As soon as the local deposits are removed, this action will stop. The velocity of flow away from the outlet decreases, roughly, faster than the square of the distance. So that, in a relatively short distance, the velocity becomes too small even to move the fine material.

Sediment flushing is not effective unless the reservoir is drawn down to an extent that flow conditions over the deposits approach that of the original river. In such a case, the erosion over the delta starts from both ends. On the downstream end, a negative step (scour) develops and it moves upstream, if the local flow is supercritical. Similarly on the upstream end, a negative step starts moving downstream. Effective sluicing of sediment would take place when both the steps meet. The celerity of bed transients (Mahmood and Ponce, 1976) is very small, so that in a long reservoir, effective flushing will require that the reservoir is appreciably drawn down for a period of several months.

Sediment flushing data on Guernsey Dam (Jarecki and Murphy, (1965), Warsak Dam (Chaudhry, 1982) and Sefidrud Reservoir (Farhoodi, 1985), are discussed below in order to bring out prototype experience.

Guernsey Dam is a multipurpose, earth-fill dam on North Platte River which was completed in 1927. The dam with a height of 41.1 m is located in a rocky canyon. The length of reservoir is 23.5 km and the mean annual flow is 0.89 km^3. Due to siltation, the capacity of the dam in 1959 had reduced by 40 percent. On the average, reservoir deposits, at that time, consisted of 17 percent sand, 61 percent silt and 22 percent clay. The average density of deposits based on gamma probe and other investigations, was measured as 1.074 tons/m^3 (which is judged to be on the low side). The reservoir is naturally drawn down every year due to withdrawals during dry periods. Sediment concentration data at 5 stations within the reservoir and one station below the dam were collected during 1959 - 62 periods of drawdown. Table 6-2 summarizes the relevant sediment sluicing data for the period when the outflow was larger than the inflow. The average sediment concentration in the release was only 182 ppm and over 34 days aggregate period, 65,000 m^3 of sediment, equivalent to 0.1 percent of the capacity, were removed.

Warsak Dam is a multipurpose, 76.m high concrete dam built in 1960 on Kabul River in Pakistan. The spillway crest level is 374.9 m and the conservation pool level is 387.1 m. The length of reservoir is 41.8 km and the catchment area is 67,340 km^2. During 1961-70, the mean annual flow at the site was 21.7 km^3 with an

GUERNSEY RESERVOIR

SEDIMENT SLUICING DATA

Period	Reservoir Level (m)	Inflow (Mm^3)	Outflow (Mm^3)	Average Sediment Release (ppm)
July 10–July 19, 1960	1342.8 – 1335.3	90.0	110.1	182
Aug. 08–Aug. 17, 1960	1342.6 – 1335.1	95.9	114.2	136
July 23–July 29, 1961	1341.3 – 1334.4	64.9	77.1	222
July 26–Aug. 02, 1962	1342.6 – 1334.4	65.2	82.2	209
TOTAL:		316.0	383.6	182

average measured suspended sediment concentration of 727 ppm. Maximum and minimum discharges during this period were observed as 4,276 and 87 m^3/s, respectively, and the maximum and minimum sediment concentrations were 19,200 and 7 ppm, respectively. Particle size distribution of measured suspended load consisted of 12% sand, 60% silt and 28% clay. Gross storage capacity of the reservoir at construction was 0.17 km^3, up to 387.1 m elevation, and the dead storage was 0.08 km^3 below the spillway crest. After first year's operation, a deposit of 0.03 km^3 was measured in the reservoir and in 5 years operation, the deposit volume amounted to about 0.07 km^3. By 1980, the reservoir had completely silted up to the conservation pool elevation, except for a 60 m by 6 m deep channel on the right bank where the power and irrigation intakes are located. The river does carry gravel and cobbles, which are not reflected in the measured load. Sediment deposits in the reservoir show accumulation of gravel, cobbles and boulders on the surface. During a site visit in 1983, it was found that gravel particles up to 75 mm are passed from the reservoir with irrigation supplies, (Mahmood, 1984).

During 1976 and 1979, five flushing operations were carried out in the reservoir by purposely lowering the pool level to the spillway crest. Total duration of flushing was 490.5 hours and it has been estimated (Chaudhry, 1982) that about 4.2 Mm^3 of deposits were cleared during the flushing. Assuming an average discharge of 1,410 m^3/s, the average sediment concentration passed through the spillway is around 1,610 ppm. The quantity of average annual sediment removal in the flushing operations is around 6.4 percent of average annual measured load.

Sluicing conditions at Warsak are a great deal more favorable than at Guernsey because the river upstream is flowing in a riverine condition over the silted reservoir. However, Chaudhry (1982) notes that it will not be possible to flush the deposits below the spillway crest level unless deeper sluices are provided.

Sefidrud Dam (Farhoodi, 1985) is a 106 m high buttress gravity dam on Ghazel Ozan River in northwest Iran. This is also a multipurpose project which was completed in 1961. The dam is situated just below the confluence of Ghazel Ozan with Shah Rud. The length of reservoir is 25 km and its capacity is 1.8 km^3. The maximum, average annual and minimum runoff for the site is 12.0, 4.5 and 1.55 km^3, respectively. The sediment load shows a similar year to year fluctuation. The maximum, average annual and minimum sediment load is 218, 50 and 13.7 million tons. The average sediment concentration is 11,000 ppm with 15 percent sand, 56 percent silt and 29 percent clay. During 1979, before annual sediment flushing operations were tried for four years (1980-1983), measurements of sediment outflow showed that the trap efficiency of the reservoir was about 70 percent.

The flushing operation implemented at Sefidrud Reservoir is more intense than the two cases discussed above. The dam is provided with outlets at three levels. The lowest, bottom outlets, are located about 9.5 m above the river bed. They have a discharge capacity of 980 m³/sec. At the end of cropping season, when the reservoir had fallen by about 30 m and power units could not be operated, all of the impounded water and inflow were released through the bottom outlets by lowering the reservoir at a rate of about 1 m/week. Flushing supplies also included the early spring runoff, which brings in high sediment concentration. The total amount of water released through the flushing period is not available. Yearwise, duration of flushing and amount of sediment released are given in Table 6-3.

Table 6-3

FLUSHING OPERATIONS AT SEFIDRUD DAM

Year	Duration of Flushing (days)	Sediment Removed (million tons)
1980	120	24
1981	90	12
1982	150	49
1983	120	63
TOTAL	480	148

It is reported that, during flushing, there was a constant danger that massive slides of sediment onto the gates may block them. Construction period coffer dam with crest level about 20 m above the river bed, limited the elevation to which sediment could be flushed from the reservoir. It is seen from Table 6-3 that, with flushing operation lasting about three months in a year, the average amount of sediment removed was 74 percent of the average annual load.

The three cases of sediment flushing described above bring out some problems inherent in this operation. The tractive force required to reentrain reservoir sediments that have been allowed to deposit is larger than that needed to prevent its deposition. This condition is more pronounced for the fine material. In reservoirs, the fine material and bed material deposits may coexists in horizontal layers, or may be intermixed. When the deposits are intermixed, or are mostly fine material, the stream power necessary to remove a given mass of sediment is much larger than that required to initially transport it. Clay layers, even a few years old, can form a stubborn bottleneck and retard flushing by creating a control section. In Sefidrud Reservoir, releasing early spring floods at low flushing levels was a decided advantage from this point of view. In reservoirs with no carry-over storage, prolonged duration flushing operations of sediment can be adopted as a routine operation, perhaps, once every few years, if the impoundment is not needed during a part of the year. As shown by both Guernsey and Sefidrud, efficacy of sediment flushing is high if the sluicing is started at a time when the reservoir is already low during its annual operation, because, effective sediment transport within the reservoir commences when the flow over the deposits approaches riverine conditions.

Sediment flushing is more effective in narrow gorge-type reservoirs. As shown by the prototype experience, flushing flows carve out a deep channel, which is initially narrower than the original river width. With periodic flushing the scoured channel will approach the pre-dam width of the river. Thus, flushing cannot remove the valley deposits. In flood-plain type of reservoirs, rejuvenation of storage is only possible up to the size of original channel.

The scouring efficiency of flushing is, herein, defined by

$$E_s = 100. V_a / Q_f \qquad (6.3)$$

where, V_a = storage volume added by flushing = $(V_2 - V_1)$; V_1, V_2 = storage capacity of reservoir before and after flushing; Q_f = volume of water used in flushing and E_s = scouring efficiency in percent. According to theoretical concepts of sediment erosion and transport, E_s is an increasing function of energy gradient between the inlet and the discharge outlet. It is also a function of the fraction of storage filled by sediment; particle size of deposits; discharge rate used during flushing and the concentration of sediment entering with reservoir inflow during the flushing operation. Values of E_s for Guernsey and Warsak are 0.017 and 0.169 percent, respectively. Water use data are not available for Sefidrud flushing operation. The scouring efficiency in this case is estimated from the particle size distribution of reservoir deposits and scoured material to be around 0.8 percent. Low values of E_s for Guernsey can be attributed to small energy gradient and for Warsak to coarse material deposits.

The effectiveness of a flushing operation can also be measured by two other parameters: the ratio of capacity added by flushing to the original live capacity of the reservoir

$$E_c = 100. V_a / V_o \qquad (6.4)$$

and a time factor, E_t, defined as the ratio between the time required by river's sediment load to refill the added capacity to that required to create it by flushing.

$$E_t = T_r / (1 - T_f) \qquad (6.5)$$

where V_o = original live capacity of the reservoir; T_r = fraction of a year that the river's sediment load will take to refill V_a and,

T_f = fraction of a year used in flushing. Based on average daily sediment load and 100 percent trap efficiency,

$$E_t = V_a / [V_g (1 - T_f)^2] \qquad (6.6)$$

where, V_g = volume of annual sediment load in terms of dry density of deposits. Maximum value of E_c is less than 100 percent, and it depends on Q_f, E_s and morphology of the reservoir expressed as ratio of channel to reservoir width. The upper limit on feasible E_t is 1.0. For E_t less than 1, it will be possible to increase the available storage volume from year to year. For E_t greater than 1, the capacity must reduce from year to year and flushing is not effective. Volume of water used in flushing can be estimated from

$$Q_f = E_s \cdot V_a / 100. \qquad (6.7)$$

This quantity will normally be unavailable for other uses at the reservoir. At Guernsey, Q_f was used for irrigation and power releases. At Warsak and Sefidrud, it was exclusively used for flushing. With high desirable values of E_s, it will not be possible to use Q_f for power generation nor, for irrigation diversions at the dam. It will be, however, available for other uses farther downstream. Based on these considerations, an economic efficiency of flushing may also be defined in terms of the cost incurred by excluding other uses for Q_f and the benefit accruing due to the gain in capacity.

Values of operation parameters for the three cases of flushing considered herein are given in Table 6-4. Ratio V_o/V_g in this table is an indicator for the seriousness of siltation problem in a reservoir. Guernsey reservoir with its present sediment inflow would not pose a critical situation. The situation prevailing at the time of reported study was a legacy of past sediment loading which gives V_o/V_g = 50, close to the value for Sefidrud.

EVALUATION OF AVERAGE ANNUAL FLUSHING EFFICIENCIES

	Reservoir		
	Guernsey	Warsak	Sefidrud
Live Storage, V_o, Km^3	0.060	0.094	1.800
Avg. Sediment Inflow, V_g Mm^3/yr	0.18 (1)	12.62	40.00
Ratio V_o / V_g, yrs	324.0 (1)	7.4	45.0
Average Capacity added by Flushing, V_a, Mm^3/yr	0.022	1.050	7.400
Water Used in Flushing, Q_f, Mm^3	127.9	622.5	n/a
Scouring Efficiency, E_s, percent	0.017	0.169	0.8 (2)
Duration of Annual Flushing, T_f, yr	0.031	0.014	0.329
Time to Refill V_f, T_r, yr	0.123	0.084	0.276
Time Factor, E_t	0.127	0.086	0.411

Notes:

1. Sediment inflow after construction of Glendo Dam, about 26 km upstream in 1957. Prior historic average = 1.2 Mm^3 per year. Old ratio V_o / V_g = 50 years.

2. Volume of water used in Sefidrud flushing is not available. E_s estimated from calibre of scoured load and particle size distribution of reservoir deposits.

3. All values are based on averge annual data for the flushings carried out in the reservoirs. Number of years is 3 for Guernsey and 4 for both Warsak and Sefidrud.

Judging from value of E_t, it appears that increasing the duration T_f, under the present conditions, would be most beneficial for Warsak, Guernsey and Sefidrud, in that order.

The flushing operations, by releasing sediment load to the downstream river channel will tend to counter the retrogression set in by the impoundment to some extent. However, due to the sudden release of large sediment slugs, channel blockage may take place and create problem of flooding and channel deterioration over the short run. On the upstream side, the flushing operation will tend to clear the backwater deposits to some extent. If the bedload comprises gravel, this action will be limited by the development of an armor layer. There are other problems related to flushing, such as, the abrasion caused by high sediment concentrations and possible blockage of outlet gates by sediment deposits. The former will require special abrasion resistant treatment for the outlet structure and possibly, periodic repairs. To prevent the blockage of gates, special protective devices should be built. A siphon inlet to cope with the blockage problem has been provided in Santo Domingo Reservoir (Krumdieck and Chamot, 1979).

Sediment Sluicing

In contrast with sediment flushing, sediment sluicing is an operational design, in which the main sediment load coming into a reservoir is released along with the flow--mostly before it can settle down. The earliest and perhaps the most successful example of sediment sluicing is the Old Aswan Dam on Nile River in Egypt.

Aswan Dam (Assiouti, 1986, Leliavsky, 1960) was originally built as a single purpose regulation structure during 1898 - 1902 to provide summer irrigation supplies to the Middle Egypt. The structural height of the dam was 38.8 m, with a length of 1.95 km and a storage capacity of 1.06 km^3. At that time, the mean annual flow of

Nile at Aswan was estimated to be 84 km³. The design of Aswan Dam was predicated on the principle that the sediment load of the river has historically formulated the main fertilizer of Egypt and that it should not be held back in the dam. This led to a pattern of operation that allowed the flood flow to be passed through without significant heading up, till most of the heavy sediment concentration in the river has passed. The measure was a gage height of 88 m at a location of 15 km downstream. The reservoir was filled in about 3 months with nearly clear water, which was then used over the next 4 months till the beginning of next year's flood. To allow the flood waters to be passed unobstructed through the dam, about 2,000 m² of sluice gates opening were provided near the river bed. The design proved to be successful and the dam was twice raised--in 1912 and 1933.

After the last raising, the structural height of the dam increased to 52.80 m, design reservoir level was raised from the original elevation 106 m to 121 m, the length increased to 2.14 km and the storage capacity to 5.6 km³. The increased capacity made it necessary to start impoundment, somewhat earlier--at the reference gage height of 90.5 m. In the final design, the dam had 180 sluices in four groups with their sill levels at the river bed elevations of 87.65, 92.00, 96.00 and 100.00 m, respectively. The sluices, with a total cross sectional area of 2,240 m², were kept fully open during flood months of July, August and September. They could pass about 6,000 m³/s during normal flood or more than twice this flow rate during a high flood. The sluices were closed in October, and the reservoir was filled to elevation 121 m. This was held constant from January to April when the river flow was sufficient to meet irrigation requirements. The storage was used upto elevation 100 m from May to Mid-July. With this regulation, the amount of siltation measured in the reservoir was insignificant. In 1960, the construction of a power house was completed and hydropower generation started at the dam. For power, the minimum reservoir level was raised to at elevation 105 m. In 1964, High Aswan Dam with a storage capacity of 157 km^3 was completed about 6 km upstream of the old dam and the reservoir level at Old Aswan Dam was lowered. In 1986, a second power house, Aswan II Power Plant has been completed at the Old Dam (Ministry of Electricity and Energy, Egypt, undated) to maximize the power production from the releases at High Dam. With the completion of the new power house, 92 of the original sluices have been plugged with concrete and the reservoir level has been lowered to elevation 110 m. During the last construction, it was noticed that about 200,000 m^3 of sediment deposit existed in front of the dam and was cleared by dredging. As the High Dam has completely cutoff the sediment supply to old dam, the old pattern of sediment sluicing is no longer relevant.

Essentially, the same principle of sediment sluicing was adopted in the design of Roseires Dam on Blue Nile in Sudan. This dam, completed in 1966, has a structural height of 68 m and a length of 13.5 km (Ministry of Irrigation and Hydro-electric Power, undated). The central concrete section, 1 km long, has 5 deep sluices 10.5 m high by 6.0 wide placed at an invert level of 435.5 m, which is the river bed level in the main channel. Away from the deep sluices, an overflow spillway is provided with a crest level of 463.7 m. This has 10 radial gates 12.0 m high by 10.0 m wide. The design reservoir level is 480.0 m. At this level, the lake is 75 km long and it has a gross storage capacity of 3.0 km^3. Live storage capacity to elevation 467 m is 2.4 km^3. In a second stage, the design reservoir level will be raised to 490.0 with a gross storage capacity of 7.4 km^3.

Average annual flow in Blue Nile is about 50 km^3 at the site. The average flood peak is 6,300 m^3/sec and the maximum recorded flood during 60-year record is 10,800 m^3/s. The design flood capacity of sluices and spillway is 18,750 m^3/s. The structures can pass 6,400 m^3/s at a reservoir level of 467.0 m.

Average annual suspended sediment load at Roseires Dam is around 121 million tons (2500 ppm). The estimated density of deposits is 1.4 ton/m^3 so that the corresponding volume of reservoir deposits would be around 87 Mm^3. Sediment load during floods is high and is reported to be 0.44 percent by volume on the average. After the recession of peak, the average concentration falls to 0.24 and then 0.13 percent by volume.

Proposed reservoir operation program for the Roseires Dam is shown in Fig. 6-6 for a median year. For 4 months, including the flood months of July, August and September, the reservoir is maintained at elevation 467. The filling to elevation 480 m takes place during the month of October and by end-May, the reservoir has fallen to elevation 467 again.

Roseires Dam was completed in 1966 and the power house was commissioned in 1971. A complete drawdown was attained in 1970. In the original design, the trap efficiency of the reservoir was estimated to be about 16 percent.

Reservoir surveys (Schmidt, 1983) in 1981 showed that the loss of capacity during 15 years amounted to 0.55 km^3 of dead storage below elevation 467 and 0.65 km^3 of usable storage between elevation 467 and 480. This amounts to an average annual loss of gross storage of 1.65 percent and a trap efficiency of 46 percent. The complete drawdown of 1970 has vitiated the average trap efficiency data, and the actual value would be somewhat higher. If the sediment load is assumed to vary as $Q^{2.5}$, a reasonable assumption, the weighted average reservoir level for the average year works out to 467.8. The corresponding value of capacity: inflow ratio is 0.014, which give the Brune's value of trap efficiency of 57 percent. This should be close to the long-term prognosis for Roseires Dam. If the design method of operation is not followed and the reservoir level is also maintained at elevation 480 m during June through September,

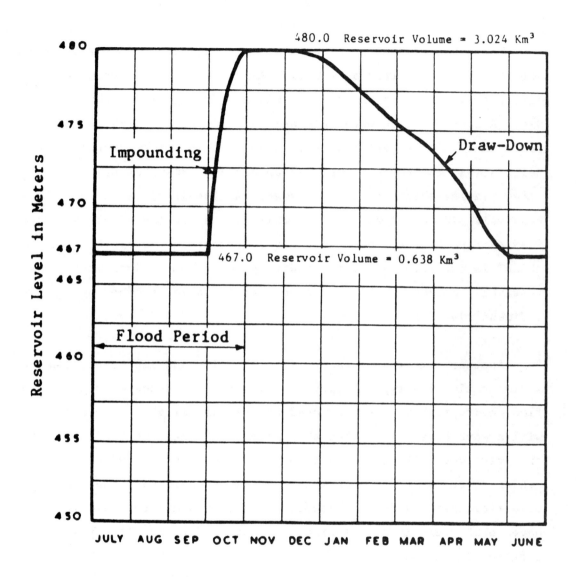

FIG. 6-6 DESIGN OPERATING PROGRAM FOR ROSEIRES DAM:
MEDIAN INFLOW AND FULL USE OF STORAGE
(After Schmidt, 1983)

the weighted average reservoir level would be close to 480 m, with Brune's trap efficiency of 83 percent. The sluices and the operation schedule are, thus, seen to save about 3.6 Mm^3 of deposit per year.

The efficacy of sediment sluicing obtained at Roseires Dam is not as high as that at the Old Aswan Dam. The key to this difference, lies in the greater width of reservoir at the Roseires Dam. A comparison between relevant data of the two dams is given in Table 6-5. It is seen that the ratio of reservoir width to maximum height (at the top of conservation pool) at Roseires Dam is five times larger than that at Old Aswan. At Roseires, even when the reservoir is operated at a lower level, a great deal of sediment load carried by the flood flows would deposit on the overbank area, which is not effected by the sluicing operation. This shows that reservoir morphology is an important variable in the design of sediment sluicing.

Another important factor in the design and implementation of sediment sluicing type of operation is the confidence with which the flow hydrograph can be predicted at the dam site. The operators will always have a fear that they might miss the opportunity to fill the reservoir if they wait too long and thus there will be a tendency to start filling the reservoir sooner than they should. Comparing the location of Roseires and Aswan dams, this problem must have been relatively minor at the latter due to its downstream location in the basin.

Density Currents

Density currents, if they develop in a reservoir, are an attractive method of ejecting high concentration of fine material. In general, the width of deposits as well as the depth of flow increases as the flow approaches the dam. The top level of deposit

98

Table 6-5

COMPARISON OF ASWAN AND ROSEIRES DAMS

	Old Aswan	Roseires
River Bed Level, m	87.5	435.5
Conservation pool level, m	121.0	480.0
Height of Conservation Pool above river bed, H, m	33.5	44.5
Mean Annual Flow, km^3	84.	50.
Capacity at Conservation Pool, km^3	5.6	3.0
Capacity:Inflow	0.067	0.060
Annual Sediment Load, Mm^3	80.0	86.6
Dam Length, L, km	2.14	13.50
L/H	63.9	303.4
Measured Trap Efficiency, percent $\simeq$	0.	46.

is also irregular across the width and a deep channel may exist in the deposit on one or both banks of the reservoir. Also, thermal stratifications, if existing, will be more pronounced close to the dam itself. All these factors introduce some uncertainty about the path that will be followed by the density current, so that it is necessary to provide multi-level, multiple outlets for aspiration of density currents. As pointed out by Bell (1942) tapping a density current requires more elaborate monitoring of thermal and salinity related stratification of reservoirs than has been done in the past.

To an extent, an advanced stage of deposits within the reservoir works against the development of density current because, the slope of deposits is smaller than the original bed of the river. Development and behavior of density currents is an area where both laboratory and prototype research can be very productive. This is discussed, along with other research needs in Chapter VII.

Sediment Dredging

The second most popular suggestion in dealing with reservoir sedimentation is that of sediment dredging. Cost of the dredging by present day techniques, which have been developed for river and harbor conditions is, however, strongly unfavorable. The cost of conventional dredging alone, without the additional cost of providing disposal areas and containment facilities, varies from $2 - 3 per m^3. The cost of replacement of storage on the other hand is about $0.12 - 0.15 per m^3. If dredged waste cannot be delivered to the downstream river channel, the cost of dredging will become even higher and the economic comparison more unfavorable.

Mechanical excavation of small reservoirs in urban setting is commonly practiced. In this case, the cost and availability of land for replacement structures is a major consideration and the waste can be used for industrial or landfill purposes so that, mechanical removal of deposits including haulage of waste by trucks is found to be economical.

In the conventional dredging methods, a major part of the cost goes in pumping the sediment-water mixture. In reservoirs, substantial hydraulic heads are available between the upstream pool and downstream river level. It should, therefore, be possible to develop newer dredging techniques for storage reservoirs that combine dust-pan type dredging with the potential energy of the reservoir to convey the dredged slurry downstream. A commercial system, that uses cutter heads, is presently available (Roveri, 1984). The price of this system will vary with location, but it may be about 3 - 4 times the cost of storage replacement indicated above. Most likely, there will be hydraulic, sedimentation and structural problems associated with large heads exceeding 100 m.

As the demand for combating reservoir sedimentation grows, technological innovations will certainly evolve and will make hydraulic dredging an economically viable solution in large reservoirs. Of all the possible alternatives, hydraulic dredging can restore the maximum amount of storage because it can treat overbank deposits which flushing and sluicing cannot handle in wide reservoirs. Also, this method under a continuous operation mode, can be used to stabilize the location of delta within the reservoir. Hydraulic dredging can also be used to clear the backwater deposits, thereby mitigating the flooding and water loss problems causes by coarse material deposits.

The scouring efficiency, E_s (Eq 6.3), for hydraulic dredging will lie between 0.25 and 0.50 percent which is much better than that possible with prolonged hydraulic flushing. It will take a smaller amount of water to remove a unit volume of deposits by dredging than by flushing.

CHAPTER VII

SUMMARY AND RESEARCH NEEDS

This monograph has been prepared to present a review of reservoir sedimentation--its worldwide extent, impacts, methods of prediction and alternatives available to mitigate the problem. A summary of the main conclusions is given herein. It is followed by a brief statement of need for research and development in the subject area.

Summary

1. One of the principal aims of water resource development is to augment the base flow in rivers. This can be economically and reliably achieved by storage reservoirs.

2. At this time (1986), the gross volume of storage reservoirs in the world is around 4,900 km^2 or roughly 13 percent of the total annual runoff. This storage is being used to augment the base flow by about 16 percent.

3. Construction of storage reservoirs saw a major growth in the 1950's. In the two decades of 50's and 60's, the gross capacity of world reservoirs increased by 25 times. Reservoir construction will continue to expand due to the increasing demand for base-flow augmentation. It is estimated that by the turn of the century, useable storage in the world will have to increase by about 2.5 fold.

4. Geologic erosion is a part of the drainage process. In the context of storage reservoirs, clastic material--the product of geologic erosion, often enhanced by human actions, is a grave

liability.

5. The world reservoirs are losing storage capacity to sedimentation at an average annual rate of about 1 percent, or about 50 km^2 per year. The cost of replacement for this loss is modestly estimated at $6 billion per year. The weighted average age of reservoir storage capacity in the world is about 22 years. The magnitude of capacity already lost is very large.

6. Genesis of clastic sediment load lies in the process of weathering. Worldwide zones of weathering have been developed and they show tht it is most active in the tropics and much less so in the temperate zone. Within various zones of weathering, climatic, geologic and tectonic factors cause large variations.

7. Weathering only prepares the parent rock for erosion. Water, as the most important agent, entrains and then transports the product to the basin outlet. Rate of erosion from a basin is strongly influenced by factors that add to the erosive power of rainfall, such as higher relief, more intense rainfall, sparse vegetal cover, tectonic disturbance and man's actions that destroy the vegetal cover and loosen the soil.

8. Not all of the clastic material eroded from a basin appears at its outlet. A drainage basin acts as a strong low-pass filter and it dampens space and time variations in the rate of erosion. Delivery ratio is a measure of the proportion of eroded material that appears at the outlet. Large basins typically deliver less than 10 percent of the eroded material. Rest of the material is stored on hillslopes, in the valleys and within stream channels. To an extent, the sediment load delivered from a basin is delimitated by the carrying capacity of the

channels.

9. Average worldwide delivery of sediment load from basins amounts
to less than a concentration of 500 ppm. However, large variations exist. Among major basins with drainage area larger than
10,000 km^2, the three largest concentrations of sediment vary
from 22,000 - 40,000 ppm., and they are all located in China.
Among various geographic regions, Oceania produces the largest
yield (about 1,000 t/km^2/yr) followed by Asia (380 t/km^2/yr),
whereas, the world average is about 165 t/km^2/yr. The lowest
sediment yield, 28 t/km^2/yr, is reported in Australia due to
its aridity, and the next higher, 38 t/km^2/yr, in Africa due to
its smaller surface runoff. Two most significant variables
correlating with sediment yield are the basin area and unit
runoff. Sediment delivery decreases roughly with 0.8 power of
drainage area and it sharply increases when the unit runoff
falls below 6 cm.

10. Human action can both increase and decrease sediment yield from
a basin. Agriculture and other activities that loosen the soil
increase sediment yield. Plain areas in Europe and USA may be
experiencing 3 - 5 times higher rates of erosion due to large
scale conversion of forest land to agricultural use. Reservoirs constructed by man, drastically decrease sediment yield
from basins. Channel stabilization also decreases sediment
yield by preventing erosion and reentrainment of valley
storage. Sediment delivery by Colorado River has diminished
from 135 to 0.1 million tons per year due to the construction
of storage reservoirs. In River Nile, 110 million tons/year
has been almost completely cutoff by High Aswan Dam and for
River Indus, it has declined from 440 to 110 million tons/year.
In Mississippi-Missouri System, the construction of dams and
channel stabilization works has decreased the sediment load by
about 50 percent.

11. Natural events, such as earthquakes, tectonic disturbancesc and volcanos can produce abnormally high sediment loads. Sediment load generated by New Madrid earthquake (1811 - 1812) in Missouri had a long-term impact on Mississippi River. A single mud-flow developing in a small sub-catchment of Kosi River in Nepal contributed about one-third of the average annual sediment load within a period of 14 hours. Mount St. Helen's eruption has increased the sediment yield of Columbia River by 4-fold.

12. It is customary and necessary to measure sediment load at or near the proposed storage sites. Many a time, sediment load measurements are not available for sufficient duration. Specialist help is needed to develop reliable estimates.

13. Simply stated, the sediment load carried by a river is deposited in the reservoir because the transport capacity of flow diminishes with decreasing velocity.

14. Sediment load can be divided into two broad categories, depending on its particle size. The fine material load comprises particles of silt and clay and, bed material load the coarser particles. This distinction was originally made necessary by sediment transport theories. It is even more valid in reservoir sedimentation. The dry density of fine material is, at least initially, much smaller than that of sand, so that the same mass of clay and silt will occupy a much larger volume of storage than would sand and gravel. The fine material also becomes highly erosion resistant with increasing age of deposit.

15. Most rivers carry more fine than bed material load. Worldwide average for fine material may be around 50 percent. Methods to predict average dry density of reservoir deposits are available. However, individual deposits will show large

variations.

16. Reservoir deposits can be described, in terms of the process of deposition, as backwater deposits, delta deposits and bottom-set deposits. The backwater deposits cause problems, such as, flooding in channel upstream of reservoir and non-beneficial water use by phreatophytes. Delta deposits and bottom-set deposits directly curtail the storage capacity of reservoirs.

17. Density currents develop in storage reservoirs when flow with large sediment concentration plunges below the surface and then flows as a distinct layer up to the reservoir. They can be used to aspirate their load through the outlets. Sediment load transported by density currents is mostly the fine material. Density currents have been observed in Lake Mead and some other reservoirs. Analytical and model study results on the behavior of density currents are available. Prototype measurements are sporadic and few.

18. Predictive methods are available for the trap efficiency of reservoirs; dry density of deposits and spatial distribution of deposits within the reservoir. These methods can be divided into two classes. The empirical methods are inductive methods based on data observed from actual storages. Analytical methods are mostly mathematical models that use equation of motion for the flow and mass conservation equation for the sediment load. Empirical methods are simple and use commonly available data. Accuracy expected from these is around 10 percent under favorable conditions. Their scope is, however, limited. For example, they cannot be used to analyze sediment flushing or sluicing operations or the particle size distribution of deposits. Mathematical models are broader in scope, but they require more detailed data as well as skilled manpower and computers. Existing mathematical models are one-dimensional

and they are based on sediment transport theories developed in rivers and canals. Experience shows that two or three mathematical models may be necessary to simulate various aspects of reservoir sedimentation. At the present state-of-the-art, it is not possible to predict micro details of sedimentation in reservoirs.

19. Given the magnitude of reservoir siltation in the world, the key question is what can be done to mitigate it. A number of methods have been tried in the past. They can be divided into three classes: methods that aim to control the sediment inflow into the reservoirs; those which try to hydraulically remove the sediment load that has already entered the reservoir and, finally, the dredging of existing deposits.

20. Watershed management is commonly suggested to reduce the sediment yield from a basin. While, watershed management is a noble activity, it cannot be very useful in alleviating reservoir sedimentation. The reason is that drainage basins store about 90 percent of eroded material, which remains available for reentrainment even after further erosion is completely cutoff. Data from a small basin in the U.S. and from Mangla watershed support this conclusion.

21. Debris dams are used to dam up one or more tributaries that contribute large sediment loads. In general, due to economy of scale, it is cheaper to provide additional storage within the main reservoir. In special cases, where mountainous streams contribute coarse material that may cause serious problems by backwater deposits, debris dams will be found to be useful.

22. Sediment bypassing can be easily practiced in off-channel storages. It has also been successfully used in small irrigation reservoirs. At other sites, they would require a

bold and innovative design that has not yet been attempted. Sediment bypassing would be difficult to achieve in streams that carry large content of fine material.

23. Sediment flushing is the practice of hydraulically eroding and discharging existing deposits in reservoirs. To be effective, it requires that the reservoir is drawn down for long periods of time. Theoretical consideration show that sediment flushing will not effect the overbank deposits and its efficacy may be reduced where even a few years old clay and silt deposits exists. New parameters defining scouring efficiency and time factor are introduced. They will provide a convenient tool to evaluate flushing operations. Two considerations will always govern sediment flushing. The amount of storage water and duration that can be exclusively devoted to flushing, and the value of time factor E_t. With the time factor less than 1, flushing can be carried out annually and will yield a cumculative improvement in storage volume. With a value greater than 1, the storage is bound to decrease from year to year in spite of flushing.

24. Sediment sluicing is an operational design in which the bulk of sediment load is released with the flow and only sediment free water is stored. It is the only method that resulted in a deposit free reservoir at Old Aswan Dam. However, in this method, the storage capacity is limited to a small fraction of the annual runoff and the reservoir operation is limited to a part of the year. Effectiveness of sluicing operation also depends on the reservoir morphology. Old Aswan Dam was successfully designed and operated to store the river flow at the tail end of the flood season, when it is nearly sediment free. Same design principle was adopted At Roseires Dam, but it has resulted in an average trap efficiency of 46 percent. The difference between Roseires and Old Aswan reservoirs is that

the former is much wider than the latter and accumulates large amount of sediment deposit in overbank areas that are not effected by sluicing.

25. Density currents, where they form, can be trapped to release fine material load. This requires a number of multiple level outlets. Exploitation of density currents also requires a more detailed monitoring of the reservoir than has been practiced so far.

26. Dredging of existing deposits is commonly suggested to reclaim the storage lost to sediment deposits. At this time (1986), conventional hydraulic dredging is about 20 times more expensive than the cost of storage replacement and is not economically viable. However, if the potential energy made available by the dam is used to obviate pumping costs, the dredging can become viable. At least, one commercial method is available whose cost may become competitive in the future.

Research Needs

As a result of the preceding review, a number of research and development problems suggest themselves. They are listed below in the order of their appearance in the preceding chapters.

Sediment Yield   Sediment load carried by the flow is the primary variable that determines the rate of sedimentation in a reservoir. This is also the first area where research is needed to improve our understanding of processes involved in the generation and delivery of sediment from large basins. The role of sediment sources and sinks has not been studied in large basins and the effect of watershed management practices has not been critically evaluated by controlled experiments. Prototype research on the fate of eroded material in its journey to the outlet and the efficacy of both structural and non-structural measures is needed. This research will enhance the possibility of controlling sediment yield from the drainage basins. A likely candidate for this research is the watershed management project area at Mangla Dam. This area has already been mapped, its relevant historic data on sediment load and land use are available and, an administrative infrastructure exists at site.

Sediment Diffusion in Deep Flows   For want of any better information, the sediment transport and deposition functions used in the mathematical modeling of reservoirs are those developed from laboratory flumes, canals and rivers. Most likely, the decay of turbulence intensity significantly changes these processes in deep reservoirs. This would be especially true of the silt and clay particles, that dominate the sediment load in rivers. Measurements of flow field and sediment concentration profiles in large reservoirs are needed to develop appropriate hydraulic and sedimentation functions.

Sediment Reentrainment   Sediment flushing is a useful method to rid of the existing deposits. It becomes more attractive when the silting up of a reservoir has reached an advanced stage. In the future, it will find a wider use as sedimentation of world reservoirs becomes worse. The efficacy of flushing depends on the rate with which the deposits can be reentrained by the flow. Existing knowledge, mostly gained from laboratory studies and theoretical investigations, suggests that rate of reentrainment in reservoirs will be strongly effected by the clay content of deposits; mineralogy of clays and the chemical regime of water. For sand particles, the rate of reentrainment depends on the velocity distribution within the reservoir and especially, that near the bed. The flow in reservoirs is strongly nonuniform, much more so than can be expected in streams. Processes of and relating to reentrainment of deposits have not been investigated in reservoirs. Prototype research in this area will be highly rewarding.

Density Currents   In the future,   reservoirs will be monitored
and operated to manage their thermal,   salinity and sediment content
in addition to the water flows.   Theoretical aspects of density
currents have been primarily developed from laboratory studies.
Their validation on prototype structures has not been attempted so
far.   Field data on sediment related density currents are scarce.
Research on the formation, behavior and fate of density currents in
reservoirs is needed.   The results will be directly useful in
alleviating the rate of sedimentation of existing reservoirs and
will help in planning and design of future structures.

Empirical Methods   Currently   available empirical methods   for
the prediction of trap efficiency and distribution of deposits are
20-30 years old.   In the meantime, an extensive data base has
developed on the gross behavior of reservoirs.   Theoretical understanding of reservoir siltation has also improved in this period.
Empirical methods will continue to be used to provide preliminary
analysis for the large and the final analysis for small projects.
The time is now right to develop a second generation of empirical
methods with expanded scope and improved accuracy.

Mathematical Models   Presently available mathematical models
for reservoir siltation are patterned after channel flow models.   In
general, the hydraulic and sedimentation processes in reservoirs are
strongly three-dimensional and stratification can have a major
effect on these processes.   Due to their speed, declining costs of
computer use and their potential to predict micro details, mathematical models will find much greater use in the future planning,
design and operation of reservoirs.   A need exists to develop more
comprehensive mathematical models than the present one-dimensional
variety.

111

REFERENCES

Armatov, K.F., Kroshkin, A.N., and Bystrov, N.N., 1974. Sediment Reservoirs in the Channels of Small Mountain Rivers, (English Trans), Soviet Hydrology, Selected Papers, AGU, Issue No. 3.

Assiouti, I.M., 1986, "History and Operation of Old Aswan Dam, Egypt," personal communication, Cairo University, Cairo,.

Bell, H.S., 1942a. Stratified Flow in Reservoirs and its Use in Prevention of Silting, Miscellaneous Publication No. 491, USDA.

---, 1942, "Density Currents as Agents for Transporting Sediments," Journal of Geology, Vol. 50, 1942.

Benjamnin, T.B., 1968, "Gravity Currents and Related Phenomena," Journal of Fluid Mechanics, Vol. 31, Part 2.

Brune, G.M., 1953, "Trap Efficiency of Reservoirs," Trans. AGU, Vol. 34, No. 3.

Camp. T.R., 1944, Discussion of Paper No. 2218, Effects of Turbulence on Sedimentation, by W.E. Dobbins, Trans. ASCE, Vol. 109.

Chaudhry, H.M., 1973, Earthquake Occurrence in the Himalayan Region and the New Tectonics, Proceedings, Seminar on Geodynamics of the Himalayan Region, National Geophysical Research Institute, Hyderabad, India.

Chaudhry, M.R., 1982, Flushing Operations of Warsak Reservoir Sediment, Paper No. 454, Proceeding, Pakistan Engineering Congress, Vol. 58, Lahore.

Chen, Y.H., Holly, F.M., Mahmood, K., and Simons, D.B., 1975. "Transport of Material by Unsteady Flow," Vol. I, Chapter 8, Unsteady Flow in Open Channels (Eds: K. Mahmood and V. Yevjevich), Water Resources Publications, Fort Collins, CO.

Churchill, M.A., 1947, Discussion of "Analysis and Use of Reservoir Sedimentation Data," by L.C. Gottschalk, Proceedings of Federal Interagency Sedimentation Conference, Denver, CO.

Cummans, J., 1981, Mudflows Resulting from the May 18, 1980 Eruption of Mount St. Helens, Washington, U.S. Geological Survey Circular 850-B, Alexandria VA, 1981.

Dorough, W.G., 1986, "Practical Problems in Using Area-Reduction-Method," personal communication, U.S. Army Engineer District, U.S. Army Corps of Engineers, Omaha, Nebraska.

Emmett, W.W., and Leopold, L.B., 1963, Downstream Pattern of Riverbed Scour and Fill, Paper No. 46, Proceedings of the Federal Inter-Agency Sedimentation Conference, Miscellaneous Publication No. 970, USDA, Washington, D.C.

Emmett, W.W., Myrick, R.M., and Meade, R.H., 1980. Field Data Describing the Movement and Storage of Sediment in East Fork River, Wyoming, USGS Open-File Report 80-1189, Denver, Colo.

Farhoodi, J., 1985, Sediment Flushing at Sefidrud Reservoir, Proceedings Second International Workshop on Alluvial River Problems, University of Roorkee, India.

Federal Inter-Agency Sedimentation Project, Some Fundamentals of Particle Size Analysis, Report No. 12, U.S. Government Printing Office, Washington, D.C.

Foley, M.G., and Sharp, R.P., 1976, General Scour and Fill along a Stream Reach, California Institute of Technology, Pasadena, Ca., (NTIS No. AD-A025 771).

Geza, Bata, and Bogich, K., 1953, Some Observations On Density Currents in the Laboratory and in the Field, Proceedings, Minnesota International Hydraulics Convention, IAHR-ASCE, Minneapolis, MN.

Goodland, R., Environmental Aspects of Hydroelectric Power and Water Storage Projects (with special reference to India), Paper presented to International Seminar, Environmental Impact Assessment of Water Resources Projects, University of Roorkee, India, 1985.

Guy, H.P., 1969, Laboratory Theory and Methods for Sediment Analysis, Techniques of Water Resources Investigations, USGS, Washington, DC.

of Water Resources Investigations, USGS, Washington, D.C.

Guy, H.P., and Norman, V.W., 1970, Field Methods for Measurement of Fluvial Sediment, Techniques of Water Resources Investigations, USGS, Washington, D.C.

Harleman, D.R.F., 1961, "Stratified Flow," Section 26, Handbook of Fluid Dynamics, V.L. Streeter, Editor-in-Chief, McGraw-Hill Book Company.

Harrison, A.S., December 1983, Deposition at the Heads of Reservoirs, U.S. Army corps of Engineers, Missouri River Division, MRD Sediment Series, No. 31.

Harrison, A.S., and Mellema, W.J., 1982, Sedimentation Aspects of the Missouri River Dams, Q54, R15, Proceedings, ICOLD, Rio de Janeiro, Brazil.

Heinemann, H. G., October 1981, "A New Sediment Trap Efficiency Curve for Small Reservoirs," Water Resources Bulletin, Vol. 17, No. 5.

Holeman, J.N., August 1968, "The Sediment Yield of Major Rivers of the World," Water Resources Research, Vol 4, No. 4.

Howard, C.S., 1953, Density Currents in Lake Mead, Proceedings, Minnesota International Hydraulics Convention, IAHR-ASCE, Minneapolis, MN.

Hurst, A.J., and Chao, P.C., September 3-5, 1975, Sediment Deposition Model for Tarbela Reservoir, Proceedings Symposium on Modeling Techniques, Modeling '75, Waterways, Harbors and Coastal Engineering Division, ASCE.

Jansen, R.B., 1980, Dams and Public Safety, A Water Resources Technical Publication, U.S. Department of Interior, Water and Power Resources Service, (USBR) Denver, CO.

Jarecki, E.A., and Murphy, T.D., 1965, Sediment Withdrawal Investigation - Guernsey Reservoir, Proceedings Federal Interagency Sedimentation Conference, ARS, Misc. Publication No. 970, USDA, Washington, D.C.

Jia-Hua, F., February 1960, " Experimental Studies on Density Currents," Scientia Sinica, Vol. IX, No. 2.

Kao, T.W., May 1977, "Density Currents and Their Applications," Journal of Hydraulic Engineering, ASCE, Vol. 103, No. HY5.

Keulegan, G.H., 1944, "Laminar Flow at the Interface of Two Liquids," Research Paper 1591, Journal of Research, National Bureau of Standards, Vol. 32.

---, November 1949, "Interfacial Instability and Mixing in Stratified Flows," Journal of Research, National Bureau of Standards, Vol. 43.

Krumdieck, A., and Chamot, P., December 1979, Sediment Flushing at the Santo Domingo Reservoir, Water Power and Dam Construction.

Kuenen, H., Ph and Migliorini, C.I., 1950, Turbidity Currents as a Cause of Graded Bedding, The Journal of Geology, Vol. 58, No. 2.

Lane, E.W., and Koelzer, V.A., 1943, Density of Sediment Deposited in Reservoirs, Report No. 9, Federal Interagency Sedimentation Project, St. Anthony Falls Hydraulics Lab, Minneapolis, MN.

Lara, J.M., and Pemberton, E.L., 1965, Initial Unit Weight of Deposited Sediments, Proceedings Federal Interagency Sedimentation Conference ARS, Misc. Publication No. 970, USDA, Washington, DC.

Leliavsky, S., 1960, Irrigation and Hydraulic Design, Vol. III, Chapman and Hall, London.

L'Vovich, M.I., 1979, World Water Resources and Their Future, (English Translation Editor: Nace, R.L.), American Geophysical Union.

Mahmood, K., 1975, Mathematical Modeling of Morphological Transients in Sand-bed Channels, Proceedings 16th Congress, IAHR, Vol 2. Sao Paulo Brazil.

Considerations, Prepared for 1975 National Water Resource Assessment, USDA (D.W. Gottlieb and Associates).

Series No. 19, U.S. Army Engineer Division, Missouri River, Corps of Engineers, Omaha, NE.

note prepared for the World Bank.

Manual, MRD Series No. 26, U.S. Army Engineer Division, Missouri River, Corps of Engineers, Omaha, NE.

Programmer's Manual, MRD Series No. 27, U.S. Army Engineer Division, Missouri River, Corps of Engineers, Omaha, NE.

U.S.AID, Islamabad, Pakistan.

Mahmood, K., and Akhtar, A.B., 1962, Artificial Cut-Off at Islam Headworks, Paper No. 352, Annual Proceedings, West Pakistan Engineering Congress, Lahore.

Mahmood, K., Dorough, W.G., and Tarar, R.N., 1979, Verification of Sediment Transport Functions on Alluvial Channel Data, Proceedings, Symposium on the Mechanics of Alluvial Channels, Lahore, Pakistan.

Mahmood, K., and Haque, M.I.,1985, Boundary Shear Stress Measurement and Analysis, Proceedings, Third US-Pakistan Binational Symposium on Mechanics of Alluvial Channels, Lahore, Pakistan.

Mahmood, K., and Ponce, V.M., April 1976, Mathematical Modeling of Sedimentation Transients in Sand-Bed Channels, Technical Report CER 75-76-KM-VMP-28, Engineering Research Center, Colorado State University, Fort Collins, CO.

McHenry, J.r., and Hawks, Paul H., 1965, Measurement of Sediment Density with Gamma Probes, Proceedings Federal Interagency Sedimentation Conference, ARS, Publication No. 970, USDA, Washington, D.C.

McHenry, J.R., Hawks, P.H., Harmon, W.C., Kelly, W. J., Gill, A.C., and Heinemann, H.G., September 1971, Determination of Sediment Density with a Gamma Probe: A Manual of Theory, Operation and Maintenance for Technical Operations Model 497, ARS 41-183, USDA.

Meade, R.H., and Parker, R.S., 1985, Sediment in Rivers of the United States, National Water Summary 1984, U.S.G.S. Water Supply Paper 2275, Washington, D.C.

Meade, R.H., Dunne, T, Richey, J.E., Santos, U.M., April 1985, and Salala, E., "Storage and Remobilization of Suspended Sediment in the Lower Amazon River of Brazil," Science, Vol. 228.

Mermal, T.W., 1970, Progress of Dam Construction in the World, World Dams Today '70, The Japan Dam Association, Tokyo.

Merrill, W.M., April 1980, Simulation of Reservoir and Lake Sedimentation, Kansas Water Research Institute, University of Kansas.

Middleton, G.V., August 1966, Experiments on Density and Turbidity Currents, Canadian Journal of Earth Sciences, Vol. 3, No. 4.

Milliman, J.D., and Meade, R.H., January 1983, "World-wide Delivery of River Sediments to Ocean," Journal of Geology, Vol. 91, No. 1.

Ministry of Electricity and Energy, undated, "Aswan II Power Plant," Arab Republic of Egypt, Cairo.

Ministry of Irrigation and Hydro-Electric Power, undated, "Roseires Dam," Khartoum, Sudan.

Pakistan Water and Power Development Authority (WAPDA) Mangla Watershed Management Study, Vol. I, 1961.

Report No. HS-7, Kalabagh Consultants, Lahore, Pakistan.

Partheniades, E., 1972, Results of Recent Investigations On Erosion and Deposition of Cohesive Sediments, Chapter 20, Sedimentation - Symposium to Honor Professor H.A. Einstein, Ed. H.W. Shen, Fort Collins, CO.

Rana, S.A., Simons, D.B., and Mahmood, K., 1973, "Analysis of Sediment Sorting in Alluvial Channels," Journal of Hydraulics Division, ASCE, Vol. 99, No. HY11.

Rehman, A., undated, "Life of Mangla Reservoir--Ways and Means of Improvement," mimeographed note, Dams Monitoring Organization, Pakistan WAPDA, Lahore.

Revio, B., June 1980, "Tamur Flood," mimeographed note; General Directorate of Hydrology and Irrigation, Kathmandu, Nepal.

Robbins, L.G., 1976, Suspended Sediment and Bed Material Studies on the Lower Mississippi River, U.S. Army Engineer District, Vicksburg, MS.

Roehl, J.W., 1962, Sediment Source Areas, Delivery Ratios and Influencing Morphological Factors, IASH Publication No. 59.

Roveri, E., 1984, "Geolidro System," Parma, Italy, personal communication.

Rubey, W.W., 1933, "Settling Velocities of Gravel, Sand and Silt," American Journal of Science, Vol. 25.

Savage, S.B., and Brimberg, J., 1975, "Analysis of Plunging Phenomena in Water Reservoirs," Journal of Hydraulic Research, Vol. 13, No. 2,

Schiff, J.B., and Schonfeld, J.C., 1953, Theoretical Considerations on the Motion of Salt and Fresh Water., Proceedings, Minnesota International Hydraulics Convention, IAHR-ASCE, Minneapolis, MN.

Schmidt, G., 1983, "Siltation Experience on Roseires Dam," Coyne et Bellier, Paris, personal communication.

Schumm, S.A., The Fluvial System, 1977, John Wiley and Sons, New York.

Sing, E.F., 1986, River Sediment Budget, Proceedings Fourth Federal Inter-Agency Sedimentation Conference, Las Vegas, Nevada.

Strakhov, N.M., 1967. Principles of Lithogenesis, Vol. I (English Tr. by Fitzsimmons, J.P.), Consultants Bureau, New York.

Toffaleti, F.B., January 1969, "Definitive Computations of Sand Discharge in Rivers, Journal of Hydraulic Engineering, ASCE, Vol. 95, No. HY1.

Trimble, S.W., May 1983, "A Sediment Budget for Coon Creek Basin in the Driftless Area, Wisconsin, 1853-1977," American Journal of Science, Vol. 283.

UNESCO, 1977, Atlas of World Water Balance, 1977, Korzoun, V.I., Editor-in-Chief, Paris.

UNESCO, 1978, World Water Balance and Water Resources of the Earth, Leningrad

Urlapov, G.A., 1977, Irrigation Reservoir That Silts Up Insignificantly, (English Trans), Soviet Hydrology, Selected Papers, AGU, Vol. 16, No. 3.

U.S. Army Corps of Engineers, July 1965, Operation Manual for the Radioactive Sediment Density Probe, U.S. Army Engineer District, Omaha, NE.

---, March 1977, Scour and Deposition in Rivers and Reservoirs, HEC-6, User's Manual, Hydrologic Engineer Center, Davis, CA.

U.S. Bureau of Reclamation, 1977, Design of Small Dams, Denver, CO.

Walters, W.H., Jr., 1975, Regime Changes of the Lower Mississippi River, M.S. Thesis, Colorado State University, Fort Collins, CO.

Williams, G.P., and Wolman, M.G., 1984, Downstream Effects of Dams on Alluvial Rivers, USGS Professional Paper 1286, Washington D.C.

Winkely, B.R., 1977, Man-Made Cut-Offs on the Lower Mississippi River, Conception, Construction and River Response, Potamology Investigations, Report 300-2, U.S. Army Engineer District, Vicksburg, MS.

Yih, S-H., 1965, Dynamics of Non-Homogeneous Fluids, Macmillan, New York.

DISTRIBUTORS OF WORLD BANK PUBLICATIONS

ARGENTINA
Carlos Hirsch, SRL
Galeria Guemes
Florida 165, 4th Floor-Ofc. 453/465
1333 Buenos Aires

AUSTRALIA, PAPUA NEW GUINEA, FIJI, SOLOMON ISLANDS, AND VANUATU
Info-Line
Overseas Document Delivery
Box 506, GPO
Sydney, NSW 2001

AUSTRIA
Gerold and Co.
A-1011 Wien
Graben 31

BAHRAIN
MEMRB Information Services
P.O. Box 2750
Manama Town 317

BANGLADESH
Micro Industries Development
Assistance Society (MIDAS)
G.P.O. Box 800
Dhaka

BELGIUM
Publications des Nations Unies
Av. du Roi 202
1060 Brussels

BRAZIL
Publicacoes Tecnicas
Internacionais Ltda.
Rua Peixoto Gomide, 209
01409 Sao Paulo, SP

CANADA
Le Diffuseur
C.P. 85, 1501 Ampere Street
Boucherville, Quebec
J4B 5E6

CHILE
Editorial Renacimiento
Miraflores 354
Santiago

COLOMBIA
Enlace Ltda.
Carrera 6 No. 51-21
Bogota D.E.

Apartado Aereo 4430
Cali, Valle

COSTA RICA
Libreria Trejos
Calle 11-13
Av. Fernandez Guell
San Jose

COTE D'IVOIRE
Centre d'Edition et de Diffusion
Africaines (CEDA)
04 B.P. 541
Abidjan 04 Plateau

CYPRUS
MEMRB Information Services
P.O. Box 2098
Nicosia

DENMARK
SamfundsLitteratur
Rosenoerns Alle 11
DK-1970 Frederiksberg C.

DOMINICAN REPUBLIC
Editora Taller, C. por A.
Restauracion
Apdo. postal 2190
Santo Domingo

EGYPT, ARAB REPUBLIC OF
Al Ahram
Al Galaa Street
Cairo

FINLAND
Akateeminen Kirjakauppa
P.O. Box 128
SF-00101
Helsinki 10

FRANCE
World Bank Publications
66 Avenue d'Iena
75116 Paris

GERMANY, FEDERAL REPUBLIC OF
UNO-Verlag
D-5300 Bonn 1
Simrockstrasse 23

GREECE
KEME
24, Ippodamou Street
Athens-11635

GUATEMALA
Librerias Piedra Santa
Centro Cultural Piedra Santa
11 calle 6-50 zona 1
Guatemala City

HONG KONG, MACAU
Asia 2000 Ltd.
6 Fl., 146 Prince Edward Road, W,
Kowloon
Hong Kong

HUNGARY
Kultura
P.O. Box 139
1389 Budapest 62

INDIA
For single titles
UBS Publishers' Distributors Ltd.
Post Box 7015
New Delhi 110002

10 First Main Road
Gandhi Nagar
Bangalore 560009

Apeejay Chambers, P.O. Box 736
5 Wallace Street
Bombay 400001

8/1-B, Chowringhee Lane
Calcutta 700016

7/188, 1(A), Swarup Nagar
Kanpur 208001

Sivaganga Road
Nungambakkam
Madras 600034

5-A, Rajendra Nagar
Patna 800016

For subscription orders
Universal Subscription Agency
Pvt. Ltd.
18-19 Community Centre Saket
New Delhi 110 017

INDONESIA
Pt. Indira Limited
Jl. Sam Ratulangi 37
Jakarta Pusat
P.O. Box 181

IRELAND
TDC Publishers
12 North Frederick Street
Dublin 1

ISRAEL
The Jerusalem Post
The Jerusalem Post Building
P.O. Box 81
Romena Jerusalem 91000

ITALY
Licosa Commissionana
Sansoni SPA
Via Lamarmora 45
Casella Postale 552
50121 Florence

JAPAN
Eastern Book Service
37-3, Hongo 3-Chome,
Bunkyo-ku 113
Tokyo

JORDAN
Jordan Center for Marketing
Research
P.O. Box 3143
Jabal
Amman

KENYA
Africa Book Service (E.A.) Ltd.
P. O. Box 45245
Nairobi

KOREA, REPUBLIC OF
Pan Korea Book Corporation
P. O. Box 101, Kwangwhamun
Seoul

KUWAIT
MEMRB
P.O. Box 5465

MALAYSIA
University of Malaya Cooperative
Bookshop, Limited
P. O. Box 1127, Jalan Pantai Baru
Kuala Lumpur

MEXICO
INFOTEC
San Fernando No. 37
Col. Toriello Guerre
Thalpan, Mexico D.F.

MOROCCO
Societe d'Etudes Marketing
Marocaine
2 Rue Moliere, Bd. d'Anfa
Casablanca

THE NETHERLANDS
Medical Books Europe, BV (MBE)
Noorderwal 38,
7241 BL Lochem

NEW ZEALAND
Hills Library and Information
Service
Private Bag
New Market
Auckland

NIGERIA
University Press Limited
Three Crowns Building Jericho
Private Mail Bag 5095
Ibadan

NORWAY
Tanum Karl Johan, A.S
P. O. Box 1177 Sentrum
Oslo 1

PAKISTAN
Mirza Book Agency
65, Shahrah-e-Quaid-e-Azam
P.O. Box No. 729
Lahore 3

PERU
Editorial Desarrollo SA
Apartado 3824
Lima

THE PHILIPPINES
National Book Store
701 Rizal Avenue
Metro Manila

PORTUGAL
Livraria Portugal
Rua Do Carmo 70-74
1200 Lisbon

SAUDI ARABIA, QATAR
Jarir Book Store
P. O. Box 3196
Rivadh 11471

SINGAPORE, TAIWAN, BURMA, BRUNEI
Information Publications
Private, Ltd.
02-06 1st Fl., Pei-Fu Industrial
Bldg., 24 New Industrial Road
Singapore

SOUTH AFRICA
For single titles
Oxford University Press
Southern Africa
P.O. Box 1141
Cape Town 8000

For subscription orders
International Subscription Service
P.O. Box 41095
Craighall
Johannesburg 2024

SPAIN
Mundi-Prensa Libros, S.A.
Castello 37
28001 Madrid

SRI LANKA AND THE MALDIVES
Lake House Bookshop
P.O. Box 244
100, Sir Chittampalam A. Gardiner
Mawatha
Colombo 2

SWEDEN
For single titles:
ABCE Fritzes Kungl.
Hovbokhandel
Regeringsgatan 12, Box 16356
S-103 27 Stockholm

For Subscription orders:
Wennergren-Williams AB
Box 30004
S-104 25 Stockholm

SWITZERLAND
Librairie Payot
6 Rue Grenus
Case postal 381
CH 1211 Geneva 11

TANZANIA
Oxford University Press
P. O. Box 5299
Dar es Salaam

THAILAND
Central Department Store
306 Silom Road
Bangkok

TRINIDAD & TOBAGO, ANTIGUA, BARBUDA, BARBADOS, DOMINICA, GRENADA, GUYANA, MONTSERRAT, ST. KITTS AND NEVIS, ST. LUCIA, ST. VINCENT & GRENADINES
Systematics Studies Unit
55 Eastern Main Road
Curepe
Trinidad, West Indies

TUNISIA
Societe Tunisienne de Diffusion
5 Avenue de Carthage
Tunis

TURKEY
Haset Kitapevi A.S.
469, Istiklal Caddesi
Beyoglu-Istanbul

UGANDA
Uganda Bookshop
P.O. Box 7145
Kampala

UNITED ARAB EMIRATES
MEMRB Gulf Co.
P. O. Box 6097
Sharjah

UNITED KINGDOM
Microinfo Ltd.
P. O. Box 3
Alton. Hampshire GU 34 2PG
England

VENEZUELA
Libreria del Este
Aptdo. 60.337
Caracas 1060-A

WESTERN SAMOA
Wesley Bookshop
P.O. Box 207
Apia

YUGOSLAVIA
Jugoslovenska Knjiga
YU-11000 Belgrade Trg Republike

ZIMBABWE
Textbook Sales Pvt. Ltd.
Box 3799
Harare